Intellectual Property, Biodiversity and Sustainable Development

Resolving the Difficult Issues

Martin Khor

Zed Books
London & New York

TWN
Third World Network
Penang, Malaysia

Intellectual Property, Biodiversity and Sustainable Development: Resolving the Difficult Issues

was first published in the United Kingdom by
Zed Books Ltd,
7 Cynthia Street,
London N1 9JF, UK
and Room 400, 175 Fifth Avenue,
New York, NY 10010, USA

and

Third World Network,
228 Macalister Road,
10400 Penang, Malaysia

in 2002.

Printed by Jutaprint
2 Solok Sungei Pinang 3, Sg. Pinang,
11600 Penang, Malaysia.

ISBN 1 84277 234 1 hb (Zed Books)
ISBN 1 84277 235 X pb (Zed Books)
ISBN 983 9747 78 9 (TWN)

A catalogue record for this book is available from the British Library.
US CIP is available from the Library of Congress.

NOTE

This book is based on a paper that was originally prepared, under the title "Intellectual Property Rights, the TRIPS Agreement and the Environment", with the financial support of the United Nations Environment Programme, to whom our deep appreciation is acknowledged.

The views expressed in this book reflect those of the author.

Contents

CHAPTER 3

CHAPTER 4

CHAPTER 5

Chapter 1

Background to the International Debate

IN recent years there has been increasing public interest in the subject of intellectual property rights (IPRs) and its relationship with sustainable development, including the environment and human development. This issue has also been the subject of rather intense debate in inter-governmental organisations, including the World Trade Organisation (WTO), the Convention on Biological Diversity (CBD), and the Food and Agriculture Organisation (FAO). Rules or provisions relating to IPRs are central to the Agreement on Trade-Related Aspects of Intellectual Property Rights (TRIPS) in the WTO, and also feature in the CBD.

The establishment of TRIPS within the WTO in 1994 signified the extension worldwide of high standards of intellectual property protection that up till then had only been applied in developed countries. TRIPS is correctly seen as a powerful legally-binding agreement, because of the strong enforcement capability backing it: member countries that do not fulfil their obligations face being brought before a WTO panel and, if found guilty, they can face trade sanctions.

Proponents of TRIPS have claimed that high standards of IPRs are required to provide adequate incentives to firms and researchers to innovate, and that such innovations give a boost to the economy. IPRs are also said to aid the process of technology transfer as they encourage foreign direct investment. They also constitute a fair system of reward to innovators and to companies that have invested in research and development, and which need to recoup their heavy expenses.

By and large, the developed countries have been the strongest promoters and defenders of TRIPS. This stems from the fact that most of the technology suppliers are companies based in the developed countries, and they hold most of the world's patents. Thus, the extension of a strong IPRs system worldwide would be to their advantage. Conversely, the developing countries are in general skeptical about the claimed benefits for them of IPRs and TRIPS. A significant number of developing countries were opposed to TRIPS being part of the Uruguay Round of negotiations which would result in the establishment of the WTO; after the subject entered the negotiating remit anyway, they tried to limit what they considered to be the more damaging aspects of the proposals that were made mainly by developed countries. Some developing countries did not participate in the negotiations, and did not realise the implications of the Agreement. Today, several years after TRIPS came into force, several officials and experts from developing countries consider that the Agreement has adverse effects on their development prospects (Correa 1998; Das 1998; Chang 2000). Consequently, many of the countries have put forward proposals in the WTO to review and revise parts of the Agreement.

The non-governmental community has been even more vocal in its criticisms of TRIPS, claiming that its implementation is having or will have negative impacts on the environment, human health, livelihood of farmers, food security and human rights. It is true that even before TRIPS was established some countries had already made certain categories of products and processes patentable. Thus, even in the absence of TRIPS, there would have developed the trends in IPRs at the national level that the NGOs find objectionable. However, it is also true that TRIPS has significantly assisted in the worldwide spread and acceleration of the higher standards and scope of IPRs protection, especially to the developing world.

The major concerns include the following. Firstly, it is said that the strong IPRs regime being established in each country through TRIPS will confer monopoly rights on private research organisations and powerful corporations. This would increase the already high concentration of economic and technological power in a few corporations, which would be able to impose higher prices for products protected by IPRs and thus obtain monopoly profits at the expense of consumers as well as smaller producers, especially those in developing countries. Since an overwhelming share of patents are held by enterprises in the developed world, there is a concern that IPRs hinder the transfer of technology to developing countries.

Secondly, whereas before the establishment of TRIPS many countries had prohibited the patenting of life forms, the provisions in TRIPS make it mandatory for WTO member countries to patent some categories of life forms and living processes. This has raised ethical, religious, environmental and development concerns.

Thirdly, there is a concern that TRIPS and IPRs, due partly to the definitions and criteria used, favour private persons or companies and modern technology. At the same time they do not recognise the crucial role traditional knowledge plays or the legitimate rights of farmers, indigenous peoples and local communities, all of whom have been major contributors to knowledge and innovations in the sustainable use of biological resources.

Fourthly, there is growing evidence of the misappropriation of traditional knowledge and the rights of farmers and local communities by the corporations and private research institutions that have been patenting biological and genetic materials and knowledge relating to their use. As the rush for patenting genes, plant varieties and medicines increases, so does evidence of "biopiracy", in which resources and knowledge of the developing world are patented by institutions of developed countries. As pointed out earlier, this development would have taken place even in the absence of TRIPS; however, TRIPS has greatly increased the number of countries which have to allow patenting of at least some biological materials and the IPRs protection of plant varieties, and thus has helped to facilitate and accelerate this trend.

Fifthly, there is the widespread fear among NGOs, farmers' groups and indigenous peoples' organisations that allowing genetic materials to be subjected to IPRs would increase the global control of a few corporations over seeds and crops, thus increasing farmers' dependence on companies for farm inputs and also reducing biodiversity as fewer varieties (some of which may also be genetically engineered) take the place of diverse traditional varieties.

In the WTO, the issue of TRIPS and the environment is one of the topics of discussion in the Committee on Trade and Environment (CTE), which had been established as part of the WTO by the GATT Ministerial Meeting in Marrakesh in April 1994 that concluded the Uruguay Round. In the CTE work programme, two issues have been identified under the item TRIPS and environment: (i) the relationship of the TRIPS Agreement with access to and transfer of technology and the development of environmentally sound technology; and (ii) the relationship between the TRIPS Agreement and multilateral environmental agreements (MEAs) which contain IPRs-related obligations. Other than the CTE, several issues relating to TRIPS, IPRs, biodiversity and the environment have been discussed in the TRIPS Council (especially in relation to the review of Article 27.3(b) of TRIPS on IPRs and biodiversity) and in the General Council (including within the context of the "problems of implementation").

Outside of the WTO, there are other international organisations or treaties that deal with the issues of traditional knowledge and biodiversity from a different perspective. The CBD was established as a response to the crisis of rapid biodiversity loss. Its overriding concerns are to conserve biodiversity, recognise the role and rights of traditional knowledge and local communities in the conservation and use of biodiversity, and to oblige countries to have equitable and fair benefit-sharing arrangements. The FAO's Commission on Genetic Resources for Food and Agriculture has been revising its International Undertaking on Plant Genetic Resources. This Undertaking is a multilateral framework to facilitate access to plant genetic resources of major crops, and benefit-sharing. It has also promoted the concept of farmers' rights, which arise from past, present and future contributions of farmers in conserving, improving and making available plant genetic resources. These rights imply that farmers should share fairly in benefits arising from the enhanced use of their genetic resources.

There is a strong perception among many NGOs and also officials of several governments that there are tensions or conflicts between the objectives, the treatment of the rights of different stakeholders, and the potential effects of the different international treaties, particularly TRIPS, the CBD and the International Undertaking. How or whether these differences can be resolved is a major area of concern and debate, including within the WTO and the CBD.

This book deals with some of the significant issues relating to the relationship between IPRs, the TRIPS Agreement, the environment and sustainable development. In defining environmental concerns, the book includes not only biodiversity and other directly environment-oriented subjects, but also the issues of traditional knowledge and the role and rights of local communities, since these are intertwined with the conservation and use of natural resources. This is in line with the now common understanding of what constitutes the environment and sustainable development, which is found for example in the CBD.

Chapter 2 examines traditional knowledge and local community rights, and how these are affected by IPRs. Chapter 3 deals with the relationship between TRIPS and the CBD, analysing their different paradigms and the points of tension between them. Chapter 4 analyses one specific aspect of TRIPS (its Article 27.3(b) that covers IPRs over living organisms and processes and plant varieties) and its implications. Finally Chapter 5 examines the issue of IPRs, TRIPS and technology transfer. In each of the chapters, some options or suggestions are given on how the issue dealt with could be followed up.

Chapter 2

TRIPS, IPRs and Traditional Knowledge

1. TRADITIONAL KNOWLEDGE AND THE LINK TO COMMUNITY RIGHTS

TRADITIONAL knowledge is now widely recognised as having played and as still playing crucial roles in economic, social and cultural life and development, not only in traditional societies but also in modern societies. This recognition has heightened in recent years as a result of the increased awareness of the environmental crisis; the role of some modern technologies, production methods and products in contributing to this crisis; and a growing appreciation that local communities (especially in developing countries) have a wide range of traditional knowledge, practices and technologies that are environmentally sound or "friendly" and that have been making use of the manifold and diverse biological and genetic resources for food, medicines and other uses. In particular, the recent increased awareness of the value of biodiversity (and the need for its conservation and sustainable use, for present and future agriculture and provision of health care) has highlighted the role and critical importance of traditional knowledge.

The knowledge of local communities, farmers and indigenous peoples on how to use the many forms and types of biological resources and for many functions, as well as on how to conserve these resources, is now recognised as being a precious resource that is critical to the future development or even survival of humankind. At the same time, this precious knowledge is maintained and thrives in the context of the traditional ways of social and economic life and customary practices of the traditional communities. The viability and sustainable development of these communities also requires their rights and access to natural resources such as land, forests and water and the preservation of the environment within which they live and work. Moreover, their rights to their knowledge, to the use of their knowledge and to the products arising from such use must also be recognised. The misappropriation of their resources, their knowledge or the products of their knowledge would not only violate their rights, but also adversely affect the conservation and use of the knowledge and of biodiversity (as the IPRs obtained by corporations and other institutions may erode the communities' rights to continue using their resources or to continue with their traditional practices).

The above summary of the position of traditional knowledge and the rights of local communities is now widely accepted. There is acknowledgement: (i) of the role and importance of traditional knowledge; (ii) that for traditional knowledge to be maintained, the social and economic context in which it developed and is applied has to be maintained; (iii) that for this context to be maintained, the rights of local communities to their resources and knowledge have to be recognised and respected; and (iv) that misappropriation of these rights can erode the basis of traditional knowledge and thus adversely affect the prospects of sustainable development.

Whilst these principles may be widely acknowledged, there are debates and disagreements on many issues, such as the interpretation of the rights of local communities and what constitutes "misappropriation". Moreover, discussions are proceeding on what measures can or should be taken, at multilateral, national or community levels, to protect and promote traditional knowledge and community rights.

2. THE VALUE OF AND THE THREATS TO TRADITIONAL KNOWLEDGE

(a) Value of Traditional Knowledge

Traditional knowledge makes valuable contributions to the two main aspects of sustainable development: the environment and the fulfilment of human needs.

There is much in traditional knowledge that has resulted in local communities engaging in environmentally sound and sustainable ways of living with and making use of the forest and its resources, and cultivating the land with plant varieties that have been chosen and evolved through many generations of farm practices and innovations. Traditional knowledge has contributed to the general knowledge on sound environmental principles and management, such as in forest conservation, soil conservation, seed conservation and crop biodiversity.

The contributions of traditional knowledge to human development, especially in food production, crop yields and health care, are also now recognised. Even today, the majority of the world's population depend on traditional knowledge and practices for food and medicines. According to RAFI (1997: p 4), 80 percent of the world's people rely on indigenous knowledge for their medical needs and half to two-thirds of the world's people depend on foods provided through indigenous knowledge of plants, animals, insects, microbes and farming systems.

The contributions of traditional knowledge to the modern economy, especially to agricultural innovation and development and the drug industry in developed countries, are also large. Pharmaceutical companies have been making use of the traditional knowledge of indigenous peoples to identify plants and their ingredients for developing new medicines. Researchers screening plants for useful substances can cut down the time taken by getting information from indigenous healers on which plants they use to treat which ailments. Companies are also collecting samples of soils identified by indigenous communities for their disease-countering properties, and thus are much better able to identify the anti-tumour, antibiotic and steroid characteristics of the fungal and bacterial organisms found in the soils (RAFI 1997). International agricultural research centres have been using plant genetic resources drawn from crops of local farming communities in developing countries to enhance agricultural biodiversity and to produce higher-yield varieties.

Quantitative estimations of the economic value are scarce, but some figures suffice to illustrate the enormity of the contribution. More than two-thirds of the world's plant species (of which at least 35,000 are estimated to have medicinal value) come from developing countries. At least 7,000 medical compounds used in Western medicine are derived from plants, and the value of germplasm from developing countries to the pharmaceutical industry in the early 1990s was estimated to be at least US$32 billion per year. Yet developing countries were paid only a fraction of this amount for the raw materials and knowledge they contribute (RAFI 1997: p vii).

In agriculture, according to one estimate cited by RAFI, genes from the fields of developing countries for only 15 major crops contribute more than US$50 billion in annual sales in the United States alone. RAFI itself also estimates that the contribution of germplasm held in the international agricultural research centres of the Consultative Group on International Agricultural Research (CGIAR) to crop production in developed countries is at least US$5 billion per annum; almost all the germplasm has been collected in developing countries. For example, the germplasm obtained in Mexico through the international maize and wheat improvement centre contributes US$2.7 billion in crop production in industrialised countries (RAFI 1997: pp 27-28).

(b) Threats to Traditional Knowledge

Traditional knowledge is facing a number of threats. A significant part of the land, forests and habitat of indigenous peoples and local communities in many countries is being affected by a combination of deforestation, logging, road construction and dam projects, mining, urbanisation, and conversion of forests to tree and agricultural plantations. The loss of resources and habitat has disrupted the social and ecological context within which the communities have made use of their traditional knowledge. Thus, the ability to maintain the knowledge or to use it is eroded.

Traditional knowledge in agriculture has also been affected in many developing countries by the conversion from biodiversity-based farming systems to monocultures promoted through the Green Revolution. In many districts in many countries, the industrial-agriculture package of hybrid seeds, chemical fertilisers, pesticides and irrigation replaced the traditional system of farming based on several different crops and many plant varieties that often also combined with fish rearing and other activities. The diversity of seed varieties for each crop, the diversity of crops themselves, as well as the diversity of different types of activities (for example, farming, fish rearing, animal rearing, traditional herb gardening) within the same farm or village, have thus been eroded. With this erosion, there was also an erosion of traditional knowledge.

In some countries, rural-to-urban migration is also taking place at a rapid pace. With the transfer of people, especially the young, the human resource base for the passing on and continued practice of traditional knowledge is being eroded.

The most complex set of problems facing the future of traditional knowledge comes from the misappropriation and potential misappropriation of this knowledge from the local communities and indigenous peoples who should be its rightful owners. In the traditional system in most countries, there has not been a system of private ownership of knowledge in relation to the use of biodiversity, i.e., farming, fishing, animal rearing, healing and the use of medicinal plants. Even in cases where there is private ownership of land or the demarcation of rights by different communities to forest areas, indigenous peoples and local communities have generally shared their knowledge of the use of seeds, medicinal plants and techniques of production, harvesting and storage, and also shared the seeds and genetic materials. Improvements of seed varieties and other innovations have also been transmitted among the farmers and transferred to other communities. There was thus free access to the genetic materials, knowledge and innovations, although of course the actual materials such as seeds or plants may be traded.

This system of cooperative innovation and community sharing is facing a challenge from the new system of knowledge rights represented by IPRs and the TRIPS regime which now forces each WTO member country to make choices as to the rights systems it would establish in relation to biological resources. Moreover, even if a country were to introduce legislation which emphasises the rights of local communities, serious challenges can nevertheless be posed if other countries establish IPRs regimes that facilitate the misappropriation of the knowledge rights of local communities of the country. This could happen if the "modern" system of IPRs places emphasis on private rights of ownership of knowledge or resources which are biased (in criteria of eligibility and in the practical process of obtaining a right) in favour of corporations or institutions that have the means and technique to obtain the rights, and at the expense of the local communities that find it difficult or impossible to meet the criteria or to participate in the process of obtaining the rights to which they should be entitled.

3. MISAPPROPRIATION OF TRADITIONAL BIODIVERSITY KNOWLEDGE, OR THE "BIOPIRACY" PHENOMENON

(a) General

Many critics of patenting of life forms have argued that it is inappropriate to use the patent system to reward scientific work in the field of biological resources and processes, as living organisms are qualitatively different from non-living materials, and knowledge relating to biological processes and materials are not "inventions." (See Chapter 4 for details.)

Some countries have already established the patenting of genetically-modified organisms as well as some types of naturally occurring organisms and their parts, including genes of animals, plants and human beings. Many of these organisms originate in the developing world.

A related problem is the patenting, usually in developed countries, of ingredients and other substances of plants for functions and uses that have already been in the public domain and in practice for many years or generations. In many cases, these are plants or substances that have been in use in a developing country or some or many developing countries. Similarly, protection in the developed countries is being granted for plant varieties the origins of whose genetic materials are in developing countries.

This phenomenon raises several issues, such as the following:

(i) The appropriation by companies or institutions of local communities' knowledge on biodiversity use transforms the rights of the communities (in most cases located in developing countries) into the private and monopoly rights of these institutions (in most cases located in developed countries). The private rights so conferred have provided the opportunity for these IPRs holders to earn revenue by virtue of their right; they can for example make a return by selling or licensing their patent to another party. Should the patent holder commercialise the products relating to the patent, it can make monopoly profits (i.e., profit additional to the profit it would have made if it did not have a patent). The local communities (and the countries they are in) that either developed or used the knowledge (and are therefore the rightful owners) would enjoy no part of the revenues or benefits arising from the patent. (Examples of corporate patenting of biological materials are provided below.)

(ii) An even more ironic situation arises if the patented process or product leads to the sale of products at relatively high prices (due to the monopoly enjoyed as a result of the patent) to developing countries, including those very countries from where the patented process or product originated. Consumers and producers in the importing developing countries would have to pay high prices for products to which these countries had actually contributed in terms of knowledge or even resource.

(iii) The institutions that have already been granted the patents in their home countries can proceed to (or simultaneously) apply for similar patents in other countries, including in the developing countries from where the knowledge originated. The local communities (or the enterprises) in the developing countries concerned would thus be constrained from making use of the patented process or making or selling the patented product. Nor can they sell in other countries where the process and product have similarly been protected by IPRs.

(iv) If the patented or otherwise protected product is a seed, there could be situations whereby the farmers of developing countries (including countries from where the original seed or gene came) may buy and use but not save and re-use the seed. They would thus incur greater costs and dependence. For example, such a situation can arise if the developing country itself has enacted IPRs laws that enable the company to patent or protect the seed variety with the stipulation that farmers buying the seed cannot save it.

(v) The phenomenon gives rise to an ironic situation of "reverse transfer of technology" in which it is the poor developing countries that are transferring knowledge and thus technology to the rich developed world. The knowledge contributes enormously to the economies and social development of the developed countries, while the developing countries get scant reward for their contribution and could likely instead end up being required to pay the institutions of the developed countries a high price (made artificially high by monopolistic IPRs) for the use of the product or process. This can also result in a large drain on the foreign exchange of the developing countries, adding to the debt problem that many of them have. The foreign-exchange outflow can be a result of the high prices paid for the imported patented products and the royalties that enterprises would have to pay to make use of the patented process.

(vi) The patenting and intellectual property protection of biological resources by private interests has the potential to restrict the ability of producers to use the processes and products relating to traditional knowledge. For example, a corporation that has successfully applied for a patent over the use of a plant for certain functions (for instance, to treat some ailments) could attempt to prevent others from using the plant for the same functions. Those who have been keeping and using (or are potential users or keepers of) traditional knowledge could thus be restricted and discouraged. If this happens, there would be an erosion of traditional knowledge and thus of the conservation and sustainable use of biodiversity.

(vii) The large-scale granting of patents for genes and other biological materials and organisms is leading to an even greater concentration of control over the world's food crops, such as maize, potato, soybean and wheat, in a few global corporations. The top five corporations involved in agricultural biotechnology (AstraZeneca, DuPont, Monsanto, Novartis and Aventis) account for 60 percent of the global pesticide market, 23 percent of the commercial seed market and virtually 100 percent of the transgenic seed market (ActionAid 1999: p 8).

(b) The General Situation on Patenting of Living Organisms

There is a great patent race taking place for genes and other biological substances. Information on this "gene patent rush" has recently been obtained by the London-based newspaper the *Guardian* (from a search conducted by GeneWatch UK) and published in its special report on"The Ethics of Genetics" (15 November 2000). Using a comprehensive commercial database, its study covered the patents on DNA sequences (partial and complete gene sequences) in 40 patent authorities worldwide including the US, European, Japanese and German patent offices.

As of November 2000, patents were pending or had been granted on more than 500,000 genes and partial gene sequences in living organisms. Of these, there were over 9,000 patents pending or granted involving 161,195 whole or partial human genes in early November 2000. The increase in this category of genes is phenomenal as the number had been only 126,672 in the previous month; thus the increase in a single month was 34,500 or 27 percent (*Guardian* 2000). The remainder of the genes on which patents were pending or had been granted were related to plants, animals and other organisms.

(c) Patenting in Agriculture

The development of the many varieties of the world's staple food crops has been carried out mainly by farmers in developing countries over the generations through cross-breeding. Until recently, plants and plant varieties were not patentable and in many countries this is still the case. This situation has changed, though, in many developed countries. In the US and Japan, patents are allowed for plant varieties. Since 1985, about 11,000 patents on plants have been registered in the US. In the European Union, patent law has been extended to micro-organisms and genes of plants, animals and humans. Thus, if a company has a patent on a gene from a rice variety, it can obtain a patent on new rice plants engineered with that gene (ActionAid 1999: p 6).

According to a study by ActionAid on biopiracy and the patenting of staple food crops, techniques to decode and identify the best plant genes are accelerating and the biotechnology industry is racing to map the genomes of the world's staple food crops with a view to patenting the vital and most interesting genes. The farmers of developing countries that developed the world's food crops would have no effective rights over the varieties that are patented by the transnational companies. According to the study: "Only 10 percent of seed is bought commercially in the developing world and many poor farmers buy seed only once in five years ... We believe the right to livelihood – a basic human right – is threatened by patents on life in food and agriculture. Our analysis is that these patents pose a threat to farmers' livelihoods and global food security. They may decrease farmers' access to affordable seed, reduce efforts in public plant breeding, increase the loss of genetic diversity and prevent traditional forms of seed and plant sharing." ActionAid suggests that patenting on these materials should cease for five years until the impact of patents on poorer farmers is assessed (ActionAid 1999: p 6).

The study also involved a search of patents on plant-related materials in various countries. It found that companies were seeking patent protection on gene sequences, proteins, plants and seeds. Three-quarters of patents on plant genes were by the private sector, and almost half of 601 patents on plant DNA were filed by just 14 multinational companies. The study commented: "Although patented plants and genes may have evolved in developing countries, there is no system of informed consent to notify the communities involved of the intentions of genetic collectors. This is the case even if the 'invention' relies upon the knowledge and insight of local people. This is characterised by countries in the developing world as '*theft*' of knowledge and natural living material."

In assessing cases of patents involving biopiracy, the study lists in two tables patents that have been claimed for naturally occurring compounds, genes or gene sequences with a variety of functions. They include:

(i) 62 patents on genes or natural compounds from plants which are traditionally grown in developing countries. The plants include rice (34 patents), cocoa (7), cassava (2), millet (1), sorghum (1), sweet potato (2), jojoba (3), nutmeg, camphor and cuphea (4), and rubber (8); and

(ii) 132 patents on genes in staple food crops which originated in developing countries but which are now grown globally. The crops include maize (68 patents), potato (17), soybean (25) and wheat (22).

Another study of biopiracy published in July 2000 by GRAIN (Genetic Resources Action International) covered 17 case studies of disputes and debates surrounding patents on food crops, animals, medicines and people. Among the cases were the following:

Patents on the Bt Gene and Bt Crops

Bacillus thuringiensis (Bt) is a naturally occurring soil bacterium which produces a protein fatal to many insects that consume it. Bt has been used as a biological pesticide by farmers since the 1940s. Companies have now genetically engineered the Bt gene into crops (including maize, soybean, cotton, potato, rice) so that the plants produce their own insecticide. The US has approved patents for Bt-maize, Bt-cotton and Bt-potato and by December 1999 there were at least 590 patents granted or pending related to Bt worldwide. Due to mergers, the technology is heavily concentrated in few hands, and some companies have obtained broad patents. For example, Belgium's Plant Genetic Systems (now owned by Aventis) was granted a US patent for "all transgenic plants containing Bt" whilst the US company Mycogen (now owned by Dow Agrosciences) obtained a European patent that covers the insertion of "any insecticidal gene in any plant." Such broad patents create huge market monopolies and thus the prospect for monopoly profits. Since Bt has already been used by farmers for over half a century as an ecological insect control system, there is a biopiracy element in the patents. Moreover Bt-crops can be environmentally harmful. Studies at Cornell University showed that pollen from Bt-maize killed monarch butterfly larvae that ingested it in the laboratory. Another study in the University of Hawaii showed insects developing resistance to many forms of the toxin in one generation, rendering Bt useless as an implanted pest control strategy. But this can also make the old Bt spray useless for organic farmers, since Bt-crops will have destroyed its effectiveness. However, despite these negative effects, the granting of patents on Bt genes and crops provides an incentive to further develop this technology (GRAIN 2000: p 5).

Patents on Soybeans

Soybean was first cultivated as a food crop in China, and is now widely used for food, oil and animal feed. The biotechnology company Agracetus was granted a very broad patent in 1994 that covered all transgenic soybeans. This led to a challenge against the patent by Monsanto on the ground that "the alleged invention lacks an inventive step" and was "not ... novel"; however, when Monsanto later bought up Agracetus and its patent, it dropped the complaint. Species patents such as this one can be used to stake claims and as a means to block research and competition. In countries where these patents are granted, farmers who use the transgenic soybeans must follow stringent rules. US farmers who use Monsanto's Roundup Ready soybeans, for example, must only use the company's own Roundup herbicide on the crop, cannot save seed for the next season, and cannot conduct research using the soybean. By December 1999, cases were brought against 475 farmers suspected by Monsanto to have saved and re-sowed seeds by Monsanto (GRAIN 2000: p 6).

Patents on Rice

Rice is the staple food for nearly half the world's population and is especially important in Asia. A GRAIN study covering the period 1982-1997 found 160 biotechnology patents on rice, most of them held by US and Japanese companies. The top 13 rice patent holders had just over half the biotechnology rice patents. In 1998, farmers in India and Thailand protested in the streets of their respective capital cities against the patenting of basmati rice (a speciality of India) and of jasmine rice (a speciality of Thailand) by a US company (MASIPAG 1998: pp 7-8).

Patents on Maize, Potato, Wheat

Research sponsored by the *Guardian* showed that as of November 2000, there were applications for patents on 2,181 maize gene sequences (the top five patenters have 85 percent of the total, including Dow with 655 gene sequences and DuPont with 587); 1,100 potato gene sequences (the top five patenters have 86 percent of the total, including Ribozyme with 796 gene sequences); and 288 wheat gene sequences (the top five patenters have 80 percent of the total, including DuPont with 117 and Monsanto with 78) (*Guardian* 2000).

Patents on Quinoa

Quinoa is an important part of the diet in the Andean countries of Latin America which has been cultivated since pre-Incan times. In 1994 a US patent was granted to two researchers from the University of Colorado, granting exclusive control of male sterile plants of the traditional Bolivian Apelawa quinoa variety and plants derived from its cytoplasm. This included 36 traditional varieties cited in the patent application. The researchers admitted they did nothing to create the male sterile variety, that it was "just part of the native population of plants ... we just picked it up", but claimed they were the first to identify and use a reliable system of cytoplasmic male sterility in quinoa for the production of hybrids. The US patent had serious implications for Bolivian farmers as the development of the hybrid quinoa would make it suitable for commercial cultivation in North America, and this would displace Bolivian exports. The patent was opposed by the Bolivian association of quinoa producers and NGOs led by RAFI. Due to this pressure, the University abandoned the patent by 1998 (GRAIN 2000: p 7).

(d) Patenting on Medicines

Just as controversial, or even more so, are patents and patent applications relating to plants that have traditionally been used for medicinal and other purposes (e.g., as an insecticide) by people in developing countries; or patents on medicines for serious ailments. Many medicines are derived from or based on biochemical compounds originating from plants and biodiversity in the tropical and sub-tropical countries. Much of the knowledge of the use of plants for medical purposes resides with indigenous peoples and local communities. Scientists and companies from developed countries have been charged with biopiracy when they appropriate the plants or their compounds from the forests as well as the traditional knowledge of the community healers, since patents are often applied for the materials and the knowledge (GRAIN 2000: p 10). The following are some examples of controversial patents.

The Turmeric Patent

Turmeric is native to the Indian sub-continent and has been used for many centuries to treat sprains, inflammatory conditions and wounds. A US patent was granted in 1995 to scientists from the University of Mississippi on the use of turmeric for healing wounds, claiming this to be novel. The patent was successfully challenged by the Indian government, which provided research papers predating the patent proving that turmeric has long been used in India to heal wounds. The US patent office then rejected the six patent claims. If not for the Indian challenge and the subsequent patent rejection, Indian companies would have been prevented from marketing turmeric for wound healing in the US. If there had been patent protection for biological resources in India, the same patent application could have been made in India and if approved the patent could have rendered illegal the use, marketing and sale of turmeric in India as a healing agent (GRAIN 2000: p 11; Oh 2000a: p 6). Although the Indian challenge in this case was successful, it is very costly to take up a legal case, or even to monitor the many thousands of patent applications for the existence of cases of abuse, and thus many such cases are likely to occur without a challenge. Systems of prevention are thus preferable.

Patents on Traditional Uses of Some South-East Asian Plants

A compilation of examples of biopiracy was made by several South-East Asian NGOs in 1998. Among the cases found were: (i) the patenting by a Japanese company of the anti-diabetic property of the banana plant, which has been used as herbal medicine in Cordillera and other parts of the Philippines to treat fever, diarrhoea, diabetes and other ailments, and other popular Filipino herbal medicines such as sambong, lagundi and takip kuhol have also been the subject of patent claims; (ii) the patenting by American scientists of a protein from a native strain of Thai bitter gourd, after Thai scientists found that compounds of the bitter gourd variety could be used against the AIDS virus; (iii) the patenting by a Japanese company of the plao-noi, a famous herbal plant used in Thailand and recorded in the country's traditional palm leaf books for centuries; (iv) the patenting by Japanese companies of the process of making *tempeh* (a unique and famously healthy food item in Indonesia), which is based on fermentation of soybeans and has been documented as a traditional food technology as early as the 16th century (MASIPAG 1998: p 6).

4. SOME VIEWS OF INDIGENOUS PEOPLES

The debate surrounding the role and the misappropriation of traditional knowledge, the implications of IPRs, and appropriate ways to protect traditional knowledge has also led representatives of indigenous communities to present their views and perspectives.

In July 1999, a group of 114 indigenous peoples' organisations from many countries around the world, as well as another 68 indigenous peoples' support groups, issued a joint indigenous peoples' statement on the TRIPS Agreement (Tebtebba Foundation 1999). Some of the key points of the statement are as follows:

- "[N]obody can own what exists in nature except nature herself... Humankind is part of Mother Nature, we have created nothing and so we can in no way claim to be owners of what does not belong to us ... [W]estern legal property regimes have been imposed on us, contradicting our own cosmologies and values."
- "We view with regret and anxiety how Article 27.3b of [TRIPS] will further denigrate and undermine our rights to our cultural and intellectual heritage, our plant, animal, and even human genetic resources and discriminate against our indigenous ways of thinking and behaving. This Article makes an artificial distinction between plants, animals, and micro-organisms and between 'essentially biological' and 'microbiological processes' for making plants and animals ... [A]ll these are life forms and life creating processes which are sacred and which should not

become the subject of proprietary ownership."

- IPRs as defined in TRIPS are monopoly rights given to individual or legal persons (e.g., transnational corporations) who can prove that the inventions or innovations they made are novel, involve an innovative step and are capable of industrial application. The application of this form of property rights over living things as if they are mechanical or industrial inventions is inappropriate. Indigenous knowledge and cultural heritage are collectively and accretionally evolved through generations. Thus, no single person can claim invention or discovery of medicinal plants, seeds or other living things.
- "The inherent conflict between these two knowledge systems and the manner in which they are protected and used will cause further disintegration of our communal values and practices." It can create divisions within indigenous communities over which individual has ownership over a particular knowledge or innovation. Furthermore, it goes against the very essence of indigenous spirituality which regards all creation as sacred.
- TRIPS "will lead to the appropriation of our traditional medicinal plants and seeds and our indigenous knowledge on health, agriculture and biodiversity conservation. It will undermine food security, since the diversity and agricultural production on which our communities depend would be eroded and would be controlled by individual, private and foreign interests. In addition, the TRIPS Agreement will substantially weaken our access to and control over genetic and biological resources; plunder our resources and territories; and contribute to the deterioration of our quality of life."
- The implementation of the TRIPS Agreement in its present form will have devastating social and environmental consequences which will be irreversible. It is an imperative, therefore, that this Agreement be amended to prohibit the patenting of life forms and the piracy of indigenous peoples' knowledge and biogenetic resources.

The indigenous peoples put forward the following proposals for the review of Article 27.3(b) of TRIPS:

(i) This Article should be amended to categorically disallow the patenting of life forms. Thus, the revised Article 27.3(b) should clearly prohibit the patenting of plants and animals including all their parts, meaning, genes, gene sequences, cells, proteins, seeds, etc. It should also prohibit the patenting of natural processes involving the use of plants, animals and other living organisms and their parts and processes used in producing variations of plants, animals and micro-organisms.

(ii) The provision for the protection of plant varieties by either a patent, a *sui generis* system, or a combination of both should be amended and elaborated further: It should:

- Disallow the use of patents to protect plant varieties.
- Ensure that the *sui generis* system which may be created will protect the knowledge and innovations and practices in farming, agriculture, health and medical care, and conservation of biodiversity of indigenous peoples and farmers.
- Build upon the indigenous methods and customary laws protecting knowledge and heritage and biological resources.
- Ensure that the protection offered to the indigenous and traditional innovation, knowledge and practices is consistent with the Convention on Biological Diversity (i.e., Articles 8j, 10c, 17.2 and 18.4) and the International Undertaking on Plant Genetic Resources.
- Allow for the right of indigenous peoples and farmers to continue their traditional practices of saving, sharing and exchanging seeds; and harvesting, cultivating, and using medicinal plants.
- Prevent the appropriation, theft and piracy of indigenous seeds, medicinal plants and the knowledge around the use of these by researchers, academic institutions, corporations, etc.
- Integrate the principle and practice of prior informed consent, which means that the consent of indigenous peoples as communities or as collectivities should be obtained before any research or collection of plants is undertaken. The right of indigenous peoples to veto any bioprospecting activity should be guaranteed. Mechanisms to enforce prior informed consent should be installed.

- Prevent the destruction and conversion of indigenous peoples' lands which are rich in biodiversity through projects like mines, monocrop commercial plantations, dams, etc., and recognise the rights of indigenous peoples to these lands and territories.

This statement was endorsed by a large number of indigenous peoples' organisations and support groups around the world, and is thus one of the most representative presentations of the views of the indigenous peoples' communities on IPRs and TRIPS to date. It is important to note not only that the signatories are of the view that the IPRs regime threatens the rights, way of life and knowledge of the indigenous peoples, but also that they reject the application of an IPRs system that confers private monopoly rights to the traditional system of indigenous peoples which is based on collective innovation and collective rights. The statement thus asserts that "no single person can claim invention or discovery of medicinal plants, seeds or other living things", that the inherent conflict between these two knowledge systems will cause further disintegration of communal values and practices (as it can create divisions within indigenous communities over which individual has ownership over a particular knowledge or innovation), and furthermore, that it goes against the very essence of indigenous spirituality which regards all creation as sacred.

The view that it is inappropriate to apply the patent or modern monopolistic IPRs system to traditional knowledge was also presented in a statement on behalf of indigenous peoples at a Roundtable on Intellectual Property and Traditional Knowledge at the World Intellectual Property Organization (WIPO) in November 1999. According to the statement: "We believe that the challenge for WIPO and governments, as well as other international multilateral organisations, is to maintain an open mind and be more daring in exploring ways and means to protect and promote indigenous and traditional knowledge outside of the dominant IPR regimes. WIPO should not insist in imposing that the IPR regime it is implementing, particularly patents, is what should be used to protect traditional knowledge. Other forms of protection should be explored and developed in partnership with indigenous peoples and other traditional knowledge holders. Any effort to negotiate a multilateral framework to protect indigenous and traditional knowledge should consider indigenous practices and customary laws used to protect and nurture indigenous knowledge in the local, national, and regional levels" (Tauli-Corpuz 1999a).

This point is further articulated by Victoria Tauli-Corpuz of the Tebtebba Foundation (Indigenous Peoples' International Centre for Policy Research and Education) in an article on the impacts of TRIPS on indigenous peoples. According to her:

"Indigenous knowledge and cultural heritage are usually collectively evolved and owned. If indigenous peoples have to use western IPRs to protect their own knowledge and innovations, they will have to identify individual inventors. This will push unscrupulous indigenous individuals to claim ownership over potentially profitable indigenous knowledge, which will cause the further disintegration of communal values and practices. It can also cause infighting between indigenous communities over who has ownership over a particular knowledge or innovation. The concept of exclusive ownership and alienability which is inherent in TRIPS will have to be internalised and imbibed by indigenous peoples even if it goes against their usual practice of making available such knowledge for the common good. The identity and survival of indigenous peoples as distinct peoples depends to a large extent on the age-old practice of common sharing of some resources, knowledge and skills which are not alienable.

"With TRIPS, indigenous peoples will now have to think of how their knowledge will be protected against so-called 'biopirates'. Sharing of knowledge becomes a dangerous proposition because it might be appropriated by those who have the capacity to use the system to claim exclusive ownership over such knowledge and commercialise it. Pharmaceutical and agri-business transnational corporations are now more aggressive in their bid to have access and control over indigenous knowledge and genetic resources which can bring them huge profits. Various bilateral agreements are forged between corporations with some national governments, some indigenous peoples' communities and organisations, and non-governmental organisations. In many cases, indigenous peoples who entered into such agreements are now finding out that they got the raw deal. This is to be expected, however, because indigenous peoples are pushed to play in a game in which the rules are defined by the opponents.

"The remaining diverse worldviews, cultural and intellectual heritage, customary laws and bio-genetic resources which provide the basis for indigenous peoples to assert their rights to self-determination are further undermined by TRIPS. It limits the options available to indigenous peoples on how to ensure that the knowledge and resources evolved collectively by them will remain in their control and primarily for their use. It undermines the ethics and practice of sharing and collective ownership because what underpins TRIPS is privatisation and commercialisation of knowledge ... The challenge, therefore, for indigenous peoples is to assert and develop further their own means of protecting their knowledge, practices and innovations so that they can continue using these for their own benefit and for others. They have to be careful not to fall into the trap of assimilating imposed western norms which are not consistent and which undermine their identities as distinct indigenous peoples" (Tauli-Corpuz 1999b).

In November 2000, the United Nations Conference on Trade and Development (UNCTAD) held an expert meeting on systems and national experiences for protecting traditional knowledge, in which several indigenous groups participated. They issued a statement of principles and recommendations. Among the principles is that: "The current Intellectual Property Rights system is inappropriate for the recognition and protection of traditional knowledge systems because of the inherent conflicts between these two systems, including: indigenous peoples' rights are holistic and collective by nature; the IPR system is founded on private, economic rights whereas indigenous peoples' systems are values-based which include both rights to use and obligations to respect the natural world; IPRs are protected within legal systems of the world, TK systems are largely unrecognised and unprotected within legal systems." Among the recommendations is that: priority must be given to strengthening of existing customary laws and value systems of indigenous peoples in the protection of traditional knowledge; patenting on life forms should be banned because it attacks the values and livelihoods of indigenous and traditional peoples; and that an indigenous peoples working group on traditional knowledge be established (and to be hosted by the UN Working Group on Indigenous Peoples) to develop mechanisms for protecting and enhancing traditional knowledge systems. Reference to "indigenous peoples" in this statement is also deemed to include traditional peoples and local communities and their cultures (UNCTAD 2000b). Many of these points have been reflected in the report of the meeting (UNCTAD 2000c).

In 1998, a statement was issued by many farmers' organisations, people's movements and NGOs in South-East Asia to the WTO Ministerial Conference held in Geneva in May. The joint statement criticised the extension of the patent system through TRIPS that gave global corporations the right to claim monopoly IPRs ownership over rice, citing specific cases. The statement made a number of demands, including that WTO member states should recognise that farmers' and community rights have precedence over IPRs and that IPRs destroy biodiversity. Member states of the Association of South-East Asian Nations (ASEAN) were urged to resist the extension of IPRs systems and instead to develop community rights at the local and national levels. The Filipino farmers-led group MASIPAG (involved in community-managed breeding and conservation efforts throughout the Philippines) helped to organise the above statement. Its own position was that its own work (involving 50 trial farms maintaining 500 collections of traditional and improved traditional varieties as well as 534 farmer-bred lines and 75 selections of rice being grown and improved by over 10,000 farmers) would be threatened by misappropriation by corporations or research agencies if TRIPS is implemented. "As far as MASIPAG is concerned, these plant varieties belong to the communities and should never be subject to private monopoly rights like IPR ... Patenting life conflicts with the values which have upheld biodiversity as part of the common history and ancestry of the Filipino people" (MASIPAG 1998).

5. OPTIONS AND ATTEMPTS TO REDRESS THE SITUATION

(a) Introduction

Given the above problems, several suggestions have been put forward to resolve the issues surrounding traditional knowledge. In considering the various suggestions, it is useful to first recognise the following points. The "crisis" of the ownership and misappropriation of traditional knowledge has arisen mainly because of the establishment of IPRs regimes (including the TRIPS Agreement but also national laws) that cover living organisms and biological resources. There are of course other causes than the IPRs regime for the erosion of traditional knowledge and its application, and these have to be dealt with in their own right. However, the recent controversies surrounding traditional knowledge have at their heart concerns that powerful corporations and other institutions are making use of the IPRs system to gain monopoly rights over research and the use and sale of biological organisms and resources as well as products such as seeds and medicines arising from the patents. On one hand there is the injustice of the resources and traditional knowledge of communities being misappropriated, and on the other hand the monopolisation leads to concentration of economic power in a few corporations that can control the global supply of seeds, food, medicines and other products. The negative results include the loss of rights (and the further marginalisation) of local communities, the erosion of the basis and maintenance of traditional knowledge, and the consequent loss of some key conditions for biodiversity conservation and its sustainable use.

In resolving this problem, a range of options can be considered. These include options that try to tackle the problem at its root (i.e., that address the inappropriateness of the IPRs system as applied to living organisms) or at least to mitigate the root problem by considering least-damaging or less-damaging policies when implementing mandatory obligations under TRIPS. Other options include ways to recognise the value of traditional knowledge and the rights of local communities that have developed and that hold the knowledge; and systems to reward the communities as part of "benefit-sharing" arrangements. The question also arises as to whether the local communities should "join the IPRs system, if you cannot beat it", or whether there can be other systems of benefit or rewards that flow from the recognition of the value of traditional knowledge and community rights. Below is a summary of some of the options for policy choices and other mechanisms.

(b) Banning the Patenting of Living Organisms

A large part of the problems surrounding the erosion of rights over traditional knowledge originated from changes in the patent laws in developed countries that in recent years have moved from a prohibition on patenting of living organisms to the rapid development of the trend of increasingly allowing the patenting of various categories of living organisms and biological processes, whether modified or naturally occurring. The extension of patentability to selected life forms and processes has now been "globalised" through TRIPS. This trend has mainly been in response to developments in biotechnology, and to pressures from the corporations involved in the industry.

Given the arguments put forward that it is inappropriate, as well as unfair, to apply the patent system to living organisms and biological processes, the option of excluding these from patentability should be seriously considered. Two levels of exclusion can be considered: that patenting of life be prohibited everywhere, or at least that each country can have the choice of exclusion in its national law. Either of these would involve an amendment in Article 27.3(b) of TRIPS: that members *shall* exclude from patentability all living organisms and biological or living processes; or that members *may* exclude these.

Should the choice of exclusion be left to each country, the concerns of misappropriation of traditional knowledge will remain if some countries, especially the developed countries, continue or accelerate their patenting of biological materials. However, the damage will at least be limited to the extent that a developing country that chooses the exclusion option can prevent such patents within its territory, and thus its people need not be prevented or constrained from making use of the materials or processes.

There are already proposals in the WTO General Council and in the TRIPS Council that the mandated review of Article 27.3(b) clarify that life forms and life processes cannot be patented. Thus the issue of the appropriateness or otherwise of patenting life forms can be seriously considered not only outside but also inside the WTO.

(c) Restricting Plant Breeders' Rights

Even if patents are prohibited, many countries provide for other types of IPRs that can also result in the same negative effects as those wrought by patents, such as private monopoly rights over plant varieties through plant breeders' rights legislation. Thus, consideration also has to be made on types of IPRs, besides patents, that can or cannot be allowed in relation to plants and other biological materials.

Most countries did not have plant breeders' rights legislation until recently. Due to TRIPS, the WTO members that previously did not have such legislation now have to consider a form of protection for plant varieties. If TRIPS is revised so that members can have the choice of excluding patenting or other protection for biological materials, then the situation reverts to the previous one, where countries were free to choose whether or not to have a system of protection for plant varieties, and what kind of system.

Even with the present TRIPS, there is considerable leeway for a member to choose its own "effective *sui generis*" system. (See subsection (d) below.)

(d) Mitigating Measures: An Appropriate Interpretation of TRIPS and *Sui Generis* Systems

It is likely that at least for several more years the TRIPS provision on living organisms will not be changed. WTO members would then face the prospect of needing to fulfil their obligations or face being called before a panel. In drawing up national legislation, countries should thus attempt to choose the most appropriate options (for example, least-damaging or less-damaging provisions) whilst remaining consistent with the TRIPS obligations. For example, at the least, national law could clarify that all naturally occurring life forms and all natural living processes are excluded from patentability; and a strong case could be made out that such a position is still consistent with obligations under TRIPS.

In respect of plant varieties, members can choose their own "effective" *sui generis* system of intellectual property protection. In selecting its system, a country can strike what it considers an appropriate balance between the rights of private breeders, the farming and local communities, and the consumers or general public. The public interest and the rights of local communities can be given their due emphasis, and the rights of private breeders can be appropriately constrained within the context of public interest. Thus, an appropriately designed *sui generis* system can affirm the role and value of traditional knowledge and the rights of farmers, indigenous peoples and local communities, as well as the interests of consumers. It can be argued that the establishment of such a *sui generis* system enables the country to protect plant varieties in a way that is "effective" in protecting local communities, farmers, the public interest, biodiversity and the environment.

(e) Prior Informed Consent from Countries of Origin

It has been proposed that one way of countering biopiracy is to grant countries of origin of biological materials or of traditional knowledge (of the use of biodiversity) the right to know that patent applications are being made in respect of the materials or knowledge, and to require that the prior informed consent of those countries be first obtained before such applications can be approved.

For this proposal to work, a provision would have to be made in patent and IPRs laws in other countries (i.e., those that are not countries of origin), including the developed countries where most patent claims are filed. To oversee the design, principles and implementation of the system, an international institutional mechanism also has to be established, with the Convention on Biological Diversity probably being the appropriate agency to host it.

In July 2000, India submitted a paper (India 2000b) on "Protection of biodiversity and traditional knowledge" to the TRIPS Council and the Committee on Trade and Environment, stating that there is a need for legal and institutional means for recognising the rights of tribal communities on their traditional knowledge based on biological resources at the international level, and to institute mechanisms for sharing of benefits arising from commercial exploitation of biological resources using such traditional knowledge. It proposed that: "Patent applicants should be required to disclose the source of origin of the biological material utilised in their invention under the TRIPS agreement and should also be required to obtain prior informed consent (PIC) of the country of origin. If this is done, it would enable domestic institutional mechanisms to ensure sharing of benefits of such commercial utilisation by the patent holders with the indigenous communities whose TK has been used." India has introduced provisions for disclosure of the source of biological material in amendments to its Patents Act, and it says that to prevent biopiracy, the acceptance of this practice of disclosure and PIC by all patent offices in the world is required.

(f) Digital Database on Traditional Knowledge

In order to counter biopiracy, information on previous and existing uses of biological resources can be compiled and published at national level, and also at international level where the various sets of national information can be compiled. Such documentation can then be used as evidence of the prior and existing knowledge on the use of biological resources, and thus be an instrument to prevent patenting of known knowledge. In this context, India is preparing an easily-navigable computerised database of documented traditional knowledge (which is already in the public domain) relating to the use of medicinal and other plants, known as the TK Digital Library (India 2000b: p 5). Such digital databases would enable patent offices all over the world to search and examine any prevalent use of prior art, and thereby prevent the grant of patents over knowledge or use that already exists.

(g) Community Registers for Traditional Knowledge

Documentation of traditional knowledge can also be done at the community level, and made available to patent offices so that they can protect the knowledge from being patented. In India, there are several projects by NGOs and research centres to compile Community Biodiversity Registers at village level. In the initiatives, the various biological resources used by the community, the uses to which they are put, and the efforts of the community in conservation are recorded (India 2000b: pp 3-5).

Community registers and national registers can be used not only as a defensive mechanism against inappropriate patenting, but also as a basis for promoting the conservation, use and transfer of traditional knowledge.

(h) Patenting of Traditional Knowledge by Local Innovators?

There have also been proposals that local communities can participate in the modern IPRs system by applying for patents for innovations developed by individuals or specific communities. Such patents have already been applied for, sometimes by a community jointly with a formal institution. Proponents of this measure argue that this would protect the local innovators and also provide a legitimate source of income.

Others point out, however, that if the innovation involves biological materials or processes, then the objections raised by many indigenous peoples' organisations (as well as by many NGOs and some governments) would apply, that the patent system is inappropriate for application to this category of materials and processes, and also that a system of individual monopoly rights is counter to the traditional values of sharing resources and knowledge. There could also be practical difficulties of distinguishing between the community-based previous and existing knowledge, and the value that is added by the innovator, and how that should be reflected in the award of the patent. Many indigenous peoples' organisations are opposed to the patenting of life, and also the attempts to incorporate traditional knowledge into the IPRs system, on the grounds that the values of the IPRs system and the traditional knowledge system are incompatible (see section on "Some Views of Indigenous peoples" above). Finally, if patenting poses several problems, there may be other, more appropriate ways of rewarding the "local innovator," such as grants, awards and prizes, and also through access and benefit-sharing arrangements.

(i) Incorporating Traditional Knowledge into TRIPS?

In October 1999, four Latin American countries (Cuba, Honduras, Paraguay and Venezuela) submitted a paper in the WTO that noted the public concerns and complaints about many cases of knowledge of local and indigenous communities being "pirated" and patented by foreign companies and researchers from abroad. They proposed that a detailed study be conducted under the TRIPS Council of how to protect the moral and economic intellectual property relating to traditional knowledge, medicinal practices and expressions of folklore of local and indigenous communities. On the basis of the study, the four countries proposed, negotiations should be initiated to establish multilateral rules to accord effective moral and economic IPRs to traditional knowledge, medicinal practices and expressions of folklore to take into account the social and collective nature of these rights

(Raghavan 1999).

It would be useful to study the desirability, practicality and implications of incorporating traditional knowledge and collective rights in an IPRs regime within TRIPS. Such a study would have to take into account the view of many indigenous peoples' organisations that the individual-based private IPRs regime is unsuitable and could cause social damage if applied to traditional knowledge. However, the proposal of the four countries seems to advocate multilateral rules that recognise the "social and collective" nature of the rights to traditional knowledge, medicinal practices and expressions of folklore. Such rights may not easily be fitted in the individual monopoly rights model of modern IPRs. Perhaps it would be more appropriate to seek multilateral rules to accord such rights to the local communities for their knowledge and practices and expressions, in appropriate ways, without necessarily labelling these as "intellectual property rights." Whether the WTO is a suitable venue for establishing such rights is also an issue for debate.

(j) Community Intellectual Rights Act/Policy

As a mechanism to protect and promote the rights of local communities over their biological resources and knowledge, a country can also enact legislation to establish such rights. The rationale for and elements of a Community Rights Act have been elaborated in some detail by Nijar (1996). A summary of the main elements of such an act is as follows (Nijar 1999c):

(i) The community is declared and recognised as the owners of community knowledge. They hold this right as custodians for past, present and future members of the community. This means the following:

   a. Their knowledge and all innovation within the community belong to the community or communities.
   b. It belongs to them in perpetuity.
   c. The community's or communities' prior informed consent must be sought for any access to their knowledge.

d. Such consent can be refused.
e. The integrity of the knowledge cannot be impaired. This means that no exclusive monopoly or similar rights can be claimed or given in respect of that knowledge. It therefore means that the knowledge is inalienable.

(ii) All elements of the culture, system and practices of communities are formally recognised. This means :

a. The entire identity and integrity of the knowledge system replete with its values, rituals and sacredness is accorded recognition.
b. This includes the practice of free exchange of knowledge and innovations between communities.

(iii) The community is entitled to allow for the commercial utilisation of its knowledge and innovation on mutually agreed terms.

(iv) If evidentiary proof of the knowledge is required, any declaration by the community in a manner and form accepted by the cultural practices of the community shall be sufficient evidence of its existence. This implies also that the onus will lie on any person contending otherwise to prove its claims.

(v) More than one community may be the owner of the knowledge and the innovation.

(vi) Any payments made for the use of the knowledge shall be paid into a fund to be co-administered by the community. The funds shall be used for, *inter alia*, the protection, development, strengthening and maintenance of the community and its knowledge and resources.

The above elements can be elaborated in a separate act, or be incorporated in other relevant acts, such as laws regulating access and benefit-sharing for biodiversity or plant varieties protection.

(k) National Legislation on Biodiversity Access and Benefit-Sharing

In fulfillment of their obligations in the CBD, countries have enacted or are drafting legislation to regulate access and benefit-sharing arrangements in relation to biodiversity and knowledge of its use. Such an act can also be an important instrument for the establishment, protection and promotion of traditional knowledge and the rights of local communities.

In the act, the sovereign right of a country over its biodiversity and knowledge can be affirmed through a clause that any party intending to make use of the country's biological resources or knowledge pertaining to them would have to first receive consent of the authorities. Obtaining resources or using knowledge without permit would be an offence. In the application process, the applicant would have to list the resource or knowledge it is seeking to use, and the prior informed consent of the local community or institution (including the state or state agencies) owning the resource or knowledge would have to be obtained. In the process of obtaining the consent, benefit-sharing arrangements should be part of the discussion. The authority could or should provide guidelines or principles for the benefit-sharing arrangements, including different types and rates of benefits.

In order to ensure that researchers or corporations do not misappropriate resources or knowledge, the act could include a provision that prior informed consent of the state and the local community has to be obtained. For this to be effectively implemented, it should be complemented by international regulation obliging all countries to require that patent applications relating to biological resources have to disclose the source of origin as well as to obtain prior informed consent from the country of origin and the local community involved. As discussed in sub-section (e) above, the CBD could be the venue for such a regulation, whilst there could be a clause introduced in TRIPS requiring that applications for such patents can be entertained only after prior informed consent has been obtained.

Under such a system, the role and rights of local communities in relation to biological resources and their uses (including elements of the local community act listed above) can be established.

(l) OAU Model Law and Convention on Community Rights and Access to Biological Resources

An interesting and influential "Draft Law and Convention on Community Rights and the Control of Access to Biological Resources" has been drawn up by the Organisation of African Unity (OAU) and approved by the OAU Summit of Leaders in May-June 1998. The draft is a model law that is meant to be used as reference by African national authorities when they draft their own national laws relating to regulation of biological resources and knowledge.

One of the interesting features of the OAU model law is that it incorporates several aspects of the inter-related issues in a single act. The law covers access to biological resources and benefit-sharing arrangements; community rights; IPRs; and protection of plant varieties. Thus, an attempt is made to incorporate the subject matter or obligations of the CBD (especially in the provisions on access and benefit-sharing and on community rights) as well as of the TRIPS Agreement (especially on the subjects of IPRs and plant varieties).

One of the chief architects of the model law, Tewolde Egziabher, has explained that the many provisions of the law are consistent with the CBD (Tewolde 1999a). The model law aims to regulate access to biological resources and community knowledge; to control access by the modern sector (mainly from the North) subject to conditions agreed to in the CBD; and to preserve the traditional access by indigenous and local communities. The conditions for access include:

- Research and development to be carried out in the country giving access.
- Prior informed consent of both the state and local communities.
- A list of other conditions to agree to before a contract is signed, including commitments to biodiversity conservation.
- Commitment to provide information and duplicate specimens to the country giving access.
- Commitment not to transfer to third parties without authorisation.
- Commitment not to patent or apply for any other IPR.
- Payment for the communal labour that has gone into creating or knowing the specific characteristic of the biodiversity or for the

knowledge or technology accessed and the work borne by the state in doing this.

- Commitment to abide by certain procedures aimed at ensuring the implementation of the mutually agreed terms.

Article 5 of the model law creates community rights and provides for the implementation of those rights. This is largely based on Articles 8(j), 10(c), 10(d) and 15.5 of the CBD. The main elements of community rights in the model law, contained in Part IV thereof, have been summarised by Tewolde and Edwards (2000). The communities have rights to:

- the protection in perpetuity (for all time) of the biological resources in their areas, their knowledge and technologies;
- grant access only after they have been given full information and weighed it in advance of granting their consent (prior informed consent);
- refuse access when they want to, and to restrict access when they feel that giving it in full could affect them negatively;
- develop, keep, use, exchange, sell or share biological resources without any interference by governments, or private natural or legal persons who claim IPRs protection; and
- obtain at least a 50 percent share of benefits obtained from any commercial use of the biological resources in their areas, or benefits obtained from their knowledge and/or technologies.

The provisions on IPRs are in Article 9, which states that "Patents over life forms and biological processes are not recognised and cannot be applied for"; and that the collector shall not apply for patents over life forms and biological processes under this legislation or any other relevant legislation.

Part V of the model law, on farmers' rights, recognises and protects these rights as stemming from the enormous contributions of farmers to conserving, developing and using plant and animal genetic resources. Farmers' varieties are recognised and shall be protected under the rules of customary practices and laws of local farming communities. Farmers' rights include the right to protect their traditional knowledge, to obtain an equitable share of benefits arising from the use of plant and animal genetic resources, to participate in decision-making at national level on policies relating to genetic resources, to save, use, exchange and sell farm-saved seed or propagating material, and to use a new breeders' variety protected under this law to develop farmers' varieties. Farmers however cannot sell farm-saved seed of a breeders' protected variety on a commercial scale (OAU 1999).

Plant breeders' rights are covered in Part VII of the model law. These rights are in recognition of efforts and investments by persons/institutions in developing new plant varieties. The plant breeders' rights comprise an exclusive right to sell (or license others to sell) plants or seeds of that variety, and to produce seeds of that variety for sale. These rights are however conditioned: they are subject to conditions on farmers' rights; and there are many exemptions, including the right of others to grow and use the plants for non-commercial purposes, and the right of farmers to save and use seed for subsequent crops (OAU 1999).

The enactment of a national law following the model could be taken as establishing a *sui generis* system that is comprehensive in scope, covering CBD obligations on access, benefit-sharing and community rights; principles of the FAO International Undertaking on farmers' rights; and IPRs and rights over plant varieties (which are topics covered by TRIPS). An issue could, however, arise with regard to the extent to which the patenting provisions in Article 9 of the model law are consistent with Article 27.3(b) of TRIPS.

(m) Non-IPRs Systems of Reward, Incentive and Benefit-Sharing

An important practical challenge is to work out systems of rewards, incentives and benefits that can be linked to individual as well as community contributions to knowledge, its maintenance and development, and that are appropriate. Such systems, which do not involve modern IPRs and which allocate rewards in accordance with the degree of contribution, would provide benefits and incentives for further development of knowledge, without misappropriating the resources and knowledge of communities.

If such systems can be drawn up and operationalised, they would be seen as good and more appropriate alternatives to IPRs. Forms of reward could include: lump-sum payments, or payments according to a percentage of sales value or profit, by collectors or users of biological resources or knowledge, to a fund established by government under access and benefit-sharing laws (with the distribution or use of the fund to include reward to local communities or innovators); and grants, awards and prizes to be given to communities and innovators.

(n) National Programmes Promoting Traditional Knowledge

Most of the proposals and measures listed above are "defensive" in that they are responding to the challenges or threats posed by TRIPS and modern IPRs systems. Should these threats be removed or significantly reduced through changes to TRIPS, or through appropriate *sui generis* systems of protection, there would, however, still be other factors eroding traditional knowledge.

Thus, in recognition of the value of traditional knowledge and the rights of local communities, there is need for a strong national programme to recognise, protect and promote traditional knowledge. If this is accorded its rightful high priority on the national agenda, the government would allocate a significant budget to facilitate such a programme. The programme could include:

- Funding and organisation of research programmes in universities, government agencies, NGOs or community organisations, to identify, record and register traditional experts in agriculture, health care, fishing, animal husbandry, etc.
- Establishing agricultural research programmes and centres for *ex situ* and *in situ* conservation of plant varieties and plant genetic resources, and for developing new plant varieties, making use of the knowledge and innovations of local farming communities, and transferring good practices and varieties throughout the country.
- Setting up or promoting herbal gardens of traditional-medicine plants.
- Ensuring adequate incomes to community healers and other community experts on traditional knowledge.

- Incorporating traditional knowledge and technologies as part of the curriculum for schools, colleges, universities and research centres.
- Incorporating traditional medicine and healing arts in state-run hospitals.
- Incorporating traditional knowledge and community rights on the programme, activities and budgets of various government ministries and agencies.
- Establishing prizes and awards recognising leaders, experts and innovations in traditional knowledge in various fields.

Chapter 3

The Relationship between TRIPS and the CBD

1. INTRODUCTION

THE relationship between the TRIPS Agreement and the Convention on Biological Diversity has been the subject of growing interest and also contention. Some analysts and representatives of some countries are of the view that there are no conflicts (or at least no serious conflicts) between the two international agreements. Some of them claim that the IPRs provisions in the CBD are consistent with WTO members' obligations in TRIPS.

Several other analysts and diplomats take the view that there are serious and inherent tensions and conflicts between the two agreements. These tensions have been the subject of several analyses (for example, Nijar 1996; Gaia and GRAIN 1998a; Tewolde 1999c; Dhar and Chaturvedi 1999) and several submissions by WTO members (especially in the Committee on Trade and Environment) as well as by member states at the CBD.

This chapter examines the IPRs provisions of the CBD, then discusses points of tension or potential conflict between TRIPS and the CBD, and finally lists some options to address these differences.

2. INHERENT TENSIONS IN THE IPRs PROVISIONS OF THE CBD

Those who are of the view that there is no conflict, or at least no inherent conflict, between TRIPS and the CBD usually point to the provisions in the CBD that directly deal with IPRs.

The provisions are in Article 16 and appear to be finely balanced.

Article 16.5 states: "Contracting parties, recognising that patents and other intellectual property rights may have an influence on the implementation of this Convention, shall cooperate in this regard subject to national legislation and international law in order to ensure that such rights are supportive of and do not run counter to its objectives."

This clause seems to recognise that IPRs can have a negative effect on implementing the CBD and that contracting parties have to cooperate to ensure that IPRs are supportive of and do not run counter to the CBD's objectives. However, this clause itself has a conditioning term, namely, that the cooperation is subject to national and international law. It is also balanced by Article 16.2.

Article 16.2 states that access to and transfer of technology to developing countries shall be provided and/or facilitated under "fair and most favourable terms, including on concessional and preferential terms where mutually agreed". In the case of technology subject to patents and other IPRs, "such access and transfer shall be provided on terms which recognise and are consistent with the adequate and effective protection of intellectual property rights. The application of this paragraph shall be consistent with paragraphs 3, 4, and 5 below."

Article 16.3 states that each contracting party shall take measures with the aim that parties (especially developing countries) that provide genetic resources are provided access to and transfer of technology which makes use of those resources, on mutually agreed terms, including technology protected by patents and IPRs, in accordance with international law and consistent with paragraphs 4 and 5.

Whilst Articles 16.5 and 16.3 place more emphasis on the obligations of developed countries with technology to facilitate the transfer of technology to developing countries (and indeed, Article 16.5 does recognise the potential negative effects of IPRs on this transfer), these articles are tempered by the need to be consistent with international law, by the terms to be "mutually agreed" to, and especially by the provision in Article 16.2 that technology access and transfer shall be on terms consistent with "adequate and effective" IPRs protection.

Whilst the aims of providing developing countries with access to technology on favourable and concessional terms are stated, the provisions on the need for consistency with IPRs protection and with international law (which presumably also includes the TRIPS Agreement) offset the obligations on technology transfer and also render the aims (of technology transfer on favourable terms) difficult to operationalise. (It should, however, be noted that the CBD came into effect before TRIPS.)

The negotiating history of the CBD explains the tensions within the various clauses in Article 16. As explained by one of the key negotiators, B.E. Tewolde of Ethiopia: "It is a complex Article because it resulted from the conflicting interests of the North, which wanted to hang on to its advantages in biotechnology, particularly genetic engineering, and the biodiversity-rich South, which wanted technology transfer in exchange. The North insisted that technology transfer should be linked to the Northern form of IPRs in order to protect the interests of their private sectors, particularly their transnational corporations. Conversely, the South wanted to make sure that IPRs do not damage the prospects for the conservation and sustainable use of its biodiversity, and insisted on the inclusion of Paragraph 5. This upset the USA so much that it became one of the reasons why it never ratified the Convention" (Tewolde and Edwards 2000).

Whilst this history explains the tensions and balancing acts inherent in Article 16, it may be argued that there is within the Article itself a basic conflict between the aim and obligation of technology transfer on preferential terms to the developing countries, and the need to recognise and be consistent with the adequate and effective protection of IPRs.

There is also a basic conflict between: (i) the recognition in Article 16.5 that patents and other IPRs can influence the CBD's implementation (and thus that parties are obliged to cooperate to ensure that IPRs support and not counter the CBD's objectives) and (ii) the clauses that this obligation be subject to international law as well as the Article 16.2 provision of the need to be consistent with effective protection of IPRs.

Insofar as the TRIPS Agreement (which came into force subsequent to the CBD) represents the main "international law" regulating the effective protection of IPRs, there is thus a conflict between TRIPS and the CBD obligations on technology transfer and on cooperation to ensure IPRs do not counter CBD objectives. Putting aside the issue of legal consistency, there is an inherent tension in spirit between the aspirations of a majority of CBD parties that recognise the potential adverse effect of a strict IPRs regime and that are demanding effective technology transfer and access, and the insistence of developed countries that the rights of IPRs holders be fully respected, irrespective of the effects on the CBD. This tension is also evident in the insistence of some countries that have maintained the position in the WTO that there is no conflict between TRIPS and the CBD.

3. OTHER TENSIONS BETWEEN TRIPS AND THE CBD

Besides the tensions inherent within Article 16 of the CBD, there are several other areas of tension between critical aspects of TRIPS and the CBD. These are examined below.

(a) Differences in Rationale, Origins and Overall Framework

There is a difference in the overall framework or objective between TRIPS and the CBD. TRIPS is an international agreement drawn up with the encouragement and active support of large corporations to promote their technological dominance and gain additional margins of profit through obtaining private monopolies. Policy makers have to decide on the balance between the rights of and benefits to IPRs holders, rival producers, and consumers. The IPRs model contained in TRIPS is tilted heavily in favour of the rights and benefits of IPRs holders. Because WTO members are obliged to fulfil TRIPS obligations, TRIPS has facilitated the extension of its particular model of IPRs to the wide membership of the WTO. WTO member countries now have to implement changes in national IPRs-related laws to reflect the TRIPS model, which promotes private monopoly rights that are expected to largely benefit transnational companies. TRIPS is basically a commercial treaty with commercial objectives that largely benefit strong private firms. The principles of environmental protection or human development are not central to TRIPS and are in fact marginalised by it, although there are references to or exemptions made on behalf of the environment, human and animal health and public order.

On the other hand, the establishment of the CBD was prompted mainly by the growing concern about the rapid worldwide loss of biodiversity, a recognition of the important role of traditional knowledge and the rights of local communities that developed and hold the knowledge, and the need to regulate access to and the sharing of benefits deriving from the conservation and sustainable use of biodiversity. The CBD therefore grew out of the concerns of the environment and development communities, which sought to emphasise the interests of the global environment and of local communities and indigenous peoples who are recognised as holding the key to biodiversity conservation and use. Thus, unlike for TRIPS, the promotion of commercial interests is not central to the objectives of the CBD, and in fact one of the CBD's central aspects is the recognition of the need to regulate the behaviour and effects of private corporations and researchers and constrain their rights of access and benefits within a larger framework that stresses the goals of environmental protection and the rights of sovereign states to their resources and the rights of local communities within them.

Many of the tensions between TRIPS and the CBD stem from these differences in the overall rationale and framework of the two regimes.

(b) National Sovereignty versus Rights of Foreign IPRs Holders

Article 3 of the CBD on "Principle" asserts that states have "the sovereign right to exploit their own resources pursuant to their own environmental policies." Article 15.1 states that: "Recognising the sovereign rights of States over their natural resources, the authority to determine access to genetic resources rests with the national governments and is subject to national legislation." Other clauses of Article 15 lay down the conditions for access (including prior informed consent) and benefit-sharing. Before the establishment of the CBD, there had not been a specific international treaty recognising the sovereign rights of a state over its genetic resources. The CBD is the first international agreement in which this principle is being made operational, and is being used to defend national interests against intrusiveness of external elements, particularly as regards bioprospecting (Tewolde and Edwards 2000: p 28). Based on this principle, countries have the right to regulate access of foreigners to biological resources and knowledge, and to determine benefit-sharing arrangements.

TRIPS enables persons or institutions to patent a country's biological resources (or knowledge relating to the resources) in countries outside the country of origin of the resources or knowledge. Moreover, under TRIPS, a WTO member must also allow foreigners to apply to patent in its country certain categories of living organisms (as well as of knowledge and processes) including those from third countries and even those originating in the member state. The national-treatment principle in Article 3 of TRIPS makes it mandatory for foreigners to have the same rights as citizens to apply for or obtain patents and other IPRs. TRIPS facilitates the conditions for the appropriation (or misappropriation) of ownership or rights over living organisms, knowledge and processes on the use of biodiversity. This appropriation is usually by researchers or corporations of developed countries over the biological materials or knowledge originating in developing countries. Even if a WTO member believes it should exclude patenting of genes and micro-organisms, and of genetically-engineered plants and animals (including such materials that originate from its own territory), it may feel constrained or unable to do so, because of the TRIPS provision. Thus, the sovereignty of developing countries over their resources, and over their right to exploit or use their resources, as well as to determine access and benefit-sharing arrangements, is compromised. This constraint on their sovereignty is notwithstanding the fact that these countries themselves became parties to TRIPS.

(c) Conflict between Private Rights of IPRs Holders and Community Rights of Traditional Knowledge Holders

In the preamble of TRIPS, it is recognised that "intellectual property rights are private rights." Under TRIPS (Article 28), a patent confers exclusive rights on its owner to prevent third parties from making, using, offering for sale, selling or importing (for these purposes) the patented product; and to prevent third parties from using the patented process (and from using, selling or importing the product obtained from the patented process). IPRs owners are taken to be natural or legal persons (such as corporations and institutions). The rights conferred are therefore to private individuals or private legal entities. Thus, in TRIPS, the award of IPRs over products or processes confers private ownership over the rights to make, sell or use the product or to use the process (or sell the products of that process). This makes it an offence for others to do so, except with the owner's permission, which is usually given only on licence or payment of royalty. Thus, IPRs often constitute obstacles to the exchange or flow of knowledge, of products of the knowledge, and their use or production.

This system of exclusive and private rights clashes with the traditional social and economic system in which local communities make use of and develop biodiversity, including crops and medicinal plants. Seeds and knowledge on crop varieties and medicinal plants are usually freely exchanged within the community. Knowledge is not confined or exclusive to individuals but shared and held collectively, and passed on and added to from generation to generation, and also from locality to locality.

Recognising the contribution and the nature of traditional knowledge, and of the indigenous and local communities that own it, the CBD has several provisions that acknowledge this and also that aim at protecting community rights. In this respect, the key Article 8(j) states that each contracting party shall "respect, preserve and maintain knowledge, innovations and practices of indigenous and local communities embodying traditional lifestyles relevant for the conservation and sustainable use of biological diversity and promote their wider application with the approval and involvement of the holders of such knowledge, innovations and practices, and encourage the equitable sharing of the benefits arising from the utilisation of such knowledge, innovations and practices." Article 15 spells out conditions for access to genetic resources, requiring that access shall be subject to prior informed consent of the contracting party providing such resources (Article 15.5). Several countries have built in the need to obtain the prior informed consent of relevant local communities, and their rights to participate in benefit-sharing arrangements.

However, the contribution and nature of community knowledge and community rights are not recognised in the TRIPS Agreement. Instead, the patent system endorsed by TRIPS favours private individuals and institutions, enabling them to acquire "rights", including rights over the products or knowledge whose development was mainly carried out by the local communities. TRIPS and the enactment of patent laws relating to biological materials in some countries have facilitated the appropriation of the knowledge and resources of indigenous and local communities, and the number of biopiracy cases has been increasing at a rapid rate. This misappropriation is counter to the principles and provisions of the CBD that oblige countries to recognise local community rights and fair benefit-sharing. Indeed, one of the main objectives of establishing the CBD was to counter the possibility of misappropriation or biopiracy, whilst one of the effects of TRIPS has been to contribute to this practice.

(d) Differing Treatment of Innovators Using Modern Technology and Traditional Knowledge

Related to the different ways in which the CBD and TRIPS treat private and community rights is the difference in their treatment of knowledge holders or innovators using modern and traditional technology. Whilst the CBD adequately recognises the nature and crucial role of traditional knowledge and practices in biodiversity conservation and use (for example, see Article 8(j) of the CBD), TRIPS is constructed in ways that effectively deny this and instead rewards additions to knowledge (even if very slight and minor) made through modern technology. This different treatment for modern technology and traditional knowledge is also associated with discrimination against local community rights.

As pointed out by Nijar (1996), the definitional constructs in TRIPS selectively favour developed countries and marginalise developing countries. The criteria for a patent claim for an invention (under Article 27.1 of TRIPS) are that it must be new, involve an inventive step and be capable of industrial application. According to Nijar (1996: pp 13-14):

> "Implicit in these requirements is that there must be an identifiable inventor. This definition almost immediately dismisses the knowledge systems and the innovations of indigenous peoples and farmers because they innovate communally, accretionally over

time, sometimes inter-generationally. Their innovations are for the common social good and are not intended for industrial application. Farmers nurture, modify and adapt their seeds over time. They freely exchange their seeds. The seeds used for breeding for the new season often [encapsulate] the genius of years of cumulative development.

"Indigenous knowledge, as is now readily acknowledged, is not passive, accidental accumulation of information on how the natural environment works. It is an organised, dynamic system of investigation and discovery that is of critical value to the sustainable maintenance of the earth's diversity.

"The TRIPS definition takes no account of the knowledge systems of the indigenous peoples. The WTO Committee on Trade and Environment frankly admits that: 'The question of new forms of protection adapted to the particular circumstances of [indigenous] peoples/communities was not raised during the TRIPS negotiations.' The TRIPS definition is based entirely on a model developed in the era of the industrial revolution to protect inventors of machineries. It denies the plural and diverse knowledge systems so vital to the preservation of the earth's resources."

(e) System of Prior Informed Consent of States and Communities (under CBD) versus Unilateral Patent Actions by Private Companies and Researchers (under TRIPS)

Article 15.5 of the CBD states that "access to genetic resources shall be subject to prior informed consent of the Contracting Party providing such resources, unless otherwise determined by that Party." Thus, intending collectors of biological resources or of knowledge relating to these have to provide sufficient information of their work and how it is intended to be used, and obtain consent, before starting the work. In the draft laws of many countries (for example, the OAU model law on community rights and access to biological resources), the prior informed consent of the state as well as the relevant local communities has to be obtained. This implies that consent can also be denied, and that consent is conditional on mutually agreed terms for benefit-sharing between the collector, the state and the local communities. The prior-informed-consent requirement is thus a measure to prevent misappropriation of resources and knowledge, and to facilitate fair benefit-sharing.

In TRIPS, there is no provision that applicants for patents or other IPRs over biological resources have to obtain prior informed consent. There is thus no recognition in TRIPS of the rights of the country in which the biological resource or knowledge of its use is located. Thus, patent applicants can submit claims on biological resources or knowledge to patent offices in any country (that recognises such patentability) and the patent offices can approve the claims without going through a process even of checking with the authorities of the country or countries of origin. Thus, whilst the CBD has established the principle and obligation of prior informed consent as a check against misappropriation or biopiracy, TRIPS, on the other hand, facilitates the possibility of such misappropriation by not recognising the need for and thus omitting a mechanism of prior informed consent.

(f) Differences in Benefit-Sharing Arrangements

A key aspect of the CBD is that it recognises the sovereign rights of states over their biodiversity and knowledge, and thus gives the state rights to regulate access, and this in turn enables the state to enforce its rights on arrangements for sharing benefits. Access, where granted, shall be on mutually agreed terms (Article 15.4) and shall be subject to prior informed consent (Article 15.5), countries providing the resources should fully participate in the scientific research (Article 15.6) and, most importantly, each country shall take legislative, administrative or policy measures with the aim of "sharing in a fair and equitable way the results of research and development, and the benefits arising from the commercial and other utilisation of genetic resources with the contracting party providing such resources. Such sharing shall be upon mutually agreed terms."

Under TRIPS, there is no provision for the patent holder, on claims involving biological resources or related knowledge, to share benefits with the state or communities in countries of origin. In fact, there is little that a country of origin can do to enforce its benefit-sharing rights (recognised in the CBD) if a person or corporation were to obtain a patent in another country based on the biological resource or related knowledge of the country of origin. It is true that a legal challenge can be launched by the state or citizens of the country of origin. However, such legal cases are expensive to take up. Even if a state has the resources to legally challenge a particular patent in another country, it may not have the resources to track down and challenge every patent that it believes to be a case of biopiracy against it. Moreover, there is no certainty that such challenges will be successful. Thus, if the patent laws, the administration of approvals or the courts of a particular country operate in a context that is favourable to the granting of such patents, there is little that can be done by a country of origin to ensure that biopiracy does not take place or that, if it takes place, it can get a remedy.

(g) Treatment of the Environment

Protection of the environment is at the heart of the rationale and provisions of the CBD. The objectives of the Convention are "the conservation of biological diversity, the sustainable use of its components and the fair and equitable sharing of the benefits arising out of the utilisation of genetic resources" (Article 1). Countries are obliged to develop strategies and plans to conserve and sustainably use biodiversity, and integrate conservation and sustainable use of biodiversity in sectoral and cross-sectoral plans and policies (Article 6); to carry out *in situ* and *ex situ* conservation (Articles 8, 9); to minimise adverse impacts on biodiversity whilst also carrying out remedial action in degraded areas (Article 10); and to conduct environmental impact assessments on and minimise adverse impacts of projects (Article 14). In particular, Article 19 asks parties to consider the need for an international biosafety protocol (which has now been established) to deal with the safety aspects of biotechnology and international transfer of genetically-modified organisms.

TRIPS does not have environmental protection as part of its objectives. Unlike the CBD, the promotion of environmental goals is not part of its rationale. It does, however, have provisions that enable members to exclude patents on environmental grounds. Article 27.2 states that "Members may exclude from patentability inventions, the prevention within their territory of the commercial exploitation of which is necessary to protect *ordre public* or morality, including to protect human, animal or plant life or health or to avoid serious prejudice to the environment, provided that such exclusion is not made merely because the exploitation is prohibited by their law." This provision provides some scope for members to take the environment into account in their patent policies.

However, there are restrictions to the terms of Article 27.2 (Nijar 1996: p 23). The commercial exploitation of the unpatentable invention must also be prohibited and on grounds as set out in the provision. The phrase "provided that such exclusion is not made merely because the exploitation is prohibited by their law" was added as concerns had been expressed that otherwise, "inventions of some products could be excluded from patentability on the grounds that the prevention of their exploitation was necessary to protect life and health pending the completion of the normal testing procedures necessary to establish their effectiveness and safety prior to the grant of marketing approval" (as per statement by the WTO, Committee on Trade and Environment, May 1995). According to Nijar (1996: p 23): "This qualification to Article 27.2 would seem to conflict directly with the precautionary principle enunciated in the CBD and which principle is expected to underpin the Biosafety Protocol. The language was also designed to harmonise with the Paris Convention which prohibits refusal of a grant of patent on the ground that the sale of the patented process is subject to restrictions or limitations imposed by domestic law."

Despite these restrictions, countries can make use of the provision to deny patents for inventions that in their opinion have adverse environmental effects. There is a strong possibility that countries that make use of this provision would face a challenge from other countries, including through the WTO dispute settlement system. The test of whether the provisions of TRIPS adequately allow members to make exclusions on environmental grounds will come if countries make use of this provision and if or when they face such challenges.

Article 27.3(b) of TRIPS also allows for exclusion from patentability of plants and animals other than micro-organisms, and essentially biological processes other than microbiological processes. Whilst the article at first reading enables the exclusion of patentability for plants and animals, in fact it has opened the door to worldwide patenting of genes and micro-organisms, and patenting of genetically-modified organisms, including modified plants and animals. Many environmental groups and scientists are concerned that patents granted on life forms would hinder the process of scientific research by researchers that do not own the patents; and also that the incentive of providing monopoly rights to companies to produce genetically-modified organisms would contribute to the proliferation of genetic-engineering applications that have adverse effects on biodiversity.

4. OPTIONS TO REDRESS THE SITUATION

There have been calls made by many parties, including several NGOs and governments, to "reconcile" the tensions or conflicts between TRIPS and the CBD. The issue of making the two agreements consistent with each other has also been discussed at the WTO, especially in the Committee on Trade and Environment and at the TRIPS Council; and at the CBD. The following discusses some of the broad options for such a "reconciliation."

(a) Maintaining the Status Quo

The first broad option is to take the approach that there are no real conflicts between TRIPS and the CBD, that in any case the two agreements should be left as they are to coexist, and that if any problems arise, they can be dealt with in an ad hoc manner on a case-by-case basis. This approach could take the view that TRIPS is a clear, legally-binding agreement with its own standing, and that the IPRs provisions in the CBD (in Article 16) clarify that whatever measures are stated therein have to be consistent with international law (including TRIPS); and therefore whatever actions are taken under the CBD have to be consistent with TRIPS. In effect, such an approach would be asking the CBD to conform to TRIPS, and (in the perspective of this approach) this conformity would resolve any tensions between the agreements.

Such an approach would however be taking a narrow view of the area of interaction between the two agreements. As the analysis above shows, there are serious differences between TRIPS and the CBD in terms of paradigm, objectives and treatment of several issues, including national sovereignty over biological resources and related knowledge, the principle and implementation of benefit-sharing, prior informed consent, and recognition of the contribution of traditional knowledge and modern technology, of individuals and communities, and of rights to be conferred in relation to these.

These differences are such that following one approach would lead to a very different outcome from following the other approach. Thus, if and when a national authority tries to take both approaches simultaneously (in an effort to fulfil the two sets of obligations), a confusing and unsatisfactory situation is likely to arise. It is also likely that since the TRIPS Agreement is simpler to put into effect and has more enforcement strength at international level, maintaining the status quo between the two agreements would lead to TRIPS having practical precedence over the CBD in terms of the effects. Already there is a fast-growing incidence of biopiracy (as discussed in Chapter 2), which is undermining the principles and effects of the CBD.

(b) Encouraging Countries to Use Their Options under TRIPS and the CBD in Favour of Sustainable Development

The second approach to reconciling the differences between TRIPS and the CBD would basically leave it to each country to interpret the agreements in ways that are most appropriate to it, maximising the creative use of provisions of each agreement to suit the country's chosen policies.

Thus, a country that wishes to conserve biodiversity and related knowledge and to protect and promote community rights, farmers' rights and traditional knowledge, as well as to assert national sovereignty and the state's rights to share benefits, could draft laws that attempt to meet these objectives whilst also remaining consistent with the obligations of TRIPS and the CBD.

Under this approach, WTO members could draft their patent laws in ways that fully take into account the flexibility enabled by the following clauses in TRIPS:

- Article 8, which states that "Members may, in formulating or amending their laws and regulations, adopt measures necessary to protect public health and nutrition, and to promote the public interest in sectors of vital importance to their socio-economic and technological development..." As pointed out by Nijar (1996: pp 20-21): "This is an important provision for including in national legislation measures in furtherance of public health and other public interests. This provision also, arguably, allows for measures protective of the innovative capacity, knowledge systems and traditional lifestyles of indigenous peoples and local communities especially if it enhances the protection of biodiversity and the sustainable use of its components. A case can be readily made [for] the critical socioeconomic value of indigenous knowledge, and this would make it WTO-legal for a country to protect and advance indigenous technology under Article 8."

- Article 27.2, which permits Members to exclude inventions from patentability on the grounds of protecting *ordre public* or morality, including to protect human, animal or plant life or health or avoid serious prejudice to the environment. There is a basis for refusing patents for those genetically-modified products which would affect human, animal or plant life or that would seriously prejudice the environment. Patents can also be refused if they offend morality; thus a case could be made that patents on life forms (or at the least some types of life forms) could be rejected on the ground that it is immoral to manipulate human life, to interfere with life forms generally or to introduce genetic material across species. Some religious groups have opposed patents on life forms on religious and ethical grounds (Nijar 1996: p 23).
- Article 27.3(b), which permits exclusion from patentability of plants and animals and of essentially biological processes. (Options relating to this are discussed in Chapter 4.)
- Article 27.3(b), which also states that members must provide for protection of plant varieties either by patents or by an effective *sui generis* system or by a combination of both. Countries have the flexibility to choose a *sui generis* system that protects traditional knowledge, farmers' rights and local community rights. (This is also discussed in greater detail in Chapter 4.)
- Article 31 provides for national legislation to grant compulsory licences, and there are no limits to the kind of grounds on which this may be done. It is legitimate to formulate in domestic law a system that grants compulsory licences for reasons such as: (a)

those set out in Article 8 (and under this, the protection of indigenous technologies and community rights); (b) where a licence is unreasonably refused to a local firm; (c) where other anti-competitive practices by patent holders are identified (Nijár 1996: pp 29-30).

Also under this approach, countries that have ratified the CBD can fulfil their obligations to protect traditional knowledge and community rights through the enactment of national legislation that covers the following areas or elements:

- Recognition of traditional knowledge.
- Local community rights in relation to resources and knowledge.
- Access and benefit-sharing in relation to biodiversity resources and knowledge relating to their use, in which the rights of the state of the country of origin, the farmers, indigenous peoples and local communities are fully taken into account.

These elements of domestic policy and legislation are discussed in other sections of this book.

A major drawback of this approach is that developing countries in general have limited capacity (in terms of policy-making, legal and administrative expertise) to analyse the international agreements and to formulate national policies and draft legislation with the sophistication required. Thus, they may not be able to make full use of the flexibilities in TRIPS and the CBD. Therefore, capacity building in this area would be required. Also, for this approach to work, developed countries would have to allow the developing countries to make use of the flexibilities in the agreements, and not unduly put pressure on them when they do so.

(c) Reforms to TRIPS and the CBD to Make Them Consistent with Sustainable-Development Objectives

A third approach would be for the international community to opt in favour of giving priority to sustainable-development goals, and amend both TRIPS and the CBD to make them more consistent with these goals. Under this approach, the spirit, objectives and main paradigm of the CBD would be the main basis of the harmonisation process, which can be operationalised using the principles of sustainable development, i.e., the protection and promotion of concerns for biodiversity and the environment, traditional knowledge, and the rights of indigenous and local communities and of the public interest.

This would require a review of TRIPS and the CBD, and suitable amendments to the relevant provisions.

For example, in a review of TRIPS (which is provided for in Articles 27.3(b) and 71), amendments can be made in Article 27.3(b) to bring the scope of exclusion of biological materials and processes in line with environmental and ethical considerations as well as the need for preventing biopiracy; and an interpretation can be made that the *sui generis* option for plant varieties can include the protection of traditional knowledge and local community rights, in line with the CBD.

As proposed by some developing countries at the WTO, Article 29 can be amended to require that applications for patents covering biological resources or knowledge on their use should be accompanied by information on the country of origin and the prior informed consent of the state and relevant local communities of that country. This would enable TRIPS to complement the access and benefit-sharing component of the CBD, in order to make it operational.

Amendments can also be made to TRIPS to strengthen the obligations of developed countries to ensure the transfer of technology to developing countries, or to operationalise the implementation of technology transfer. Consideration can also be given to revising TRIPS to allow for the exclusion or relaxation of standards of IPRs relating to environmentally sound technologies and technologies that relate to the use of biodiversity. This would bring TRIPS more in line with the spirit of the CBD, including the Article 16 provisions, such as those dealing with technology transfer on concessional and preferential terms (para 2) and with the need to ensure that IPRs are supportive of and do not run counter to CBD objectives (para 5).

In a review of the CBD, Article 16 could be amended to remove the tensions therein, so that the important objectives and principles of access to and transfer of technology to developing countries are not so constrained, as in the present CBD, by the references to the need to be consistent with adequate and effective protection of IPRs and international law. The obligations on technology transfer can also be strengthened and the implementation made more operational.

It should also be recognised that the present provisions in the CBD on access to genetic resources now place the onus of implementation on national policies and legislation. However, measures by national authorities are insufficient to enable effective implementation of access and benefit-sharing arrangements. For example, in its national legislation, the state of a country of origin may require as part of its access contract that the collector cannot patent the product or knowledge (or that such a patent can be applied for only under certain conditions or benefit-sharing arrangement); but that state would require the cooperation of patent authorities or biodiversity authorities of other states to be able to monitor or effectively implement that contract. An international protocol could be established to set guidelines and standards for access and for fair and equitable sharing of benefits, as well as to foster international cooperation to facilitate implementation of the access and benefit-sharing arrangements.

Chapter 4

TRIPS and Article 27.3(b)

1. INTRODUCTION

ARTICLE 27.3(b) of the TRIPS Agreement has aroused significant public controversy. It is also one of the most contentious issues in the WTO TRIPS Council. This Article is also often referred to in discussions within the CBD on IPRs and on the CBD-WTO relationship. The Article is at the core of debates surrounding the patenting of life forms, the effects of IPRs on local community rights and the environmental effects of IPRs.

Article 27.3(b) states: "Members may also exclude from patentability plants and animals other than micro-organisms, and essentially biological processes for the production of plants and animals other than non-biological and microbiological processes. However, members shall provide for the protection of plant varieties either by patents or by an effective *sui generis* system or by any combination thereof. The provisions of this subparagraph shall be reviewed four years after the date of entry into force of the WTO Agreement."

This subparagraph is rich with implications for such issues as the nature, evolution and ownership of knowledge in the use of biodiversity, the sharing of benefits derived from the use of biodiversity, the nature of "invention" in matters relating to nature and biological processes and products (life forms), the rights of local communities, and the ecological, social and ethical impacts of modern biotechnology (in particular, genetic engineering).

The key aspects of this Article are as follows: (i) the option to exclude from patentability certain biological organisms but not others; (ii) the option to exclude from patentability certain processes but not others; (iii) the option for protecting plant varieties through patenting or a *sui generis* system or a combination of the two; (iv) a review process for this subparagraph.

The subparagraph can be open to different interpretations in its various parts. Some issues and interpretations are examined below.

2. PATENTABILITY OF LIVING ORGANISMS AND PROCESSES: DISTINCTIONS BETWEEN PLANTS, ANIMALS AND MICRO-ORGANISMS; AND BETWEEN BIOLOGICAL AND MICROBIOLOGICAL PROCESSES

Article 27.3(b) apparently allows members to exclude from patentability plants and animals, but not micro-organisms. This has given rise to lack of clarity and indeed to considerable confusion. It is unclear why such a distinction was made between these three categories of organisms. It is also unclear whether: (i) the exclusion for plants and animals applies only to naturally occurring plants and animals, or whether members can exercise the option of exclusion to also cover plants and animals that have been genetically modified or that contain parts (including micro-organisms) that have been genetically modified; (ii) the mandatory requirement to patent micro-organisms applies only to genetically-modified micro-organisms or whether it applies also to naturally occurring micro-organisms.

Given this lack of clarity, members are able to have some flexibility in interpretation and in establishing their relevant laws. According to Article 27.1, patents shall be granted to protect inventions, whether products or processes, which are "new, involve an inventive step and are capable of industrial application." As pointed out by an Expert Group on the TRIPS Agreement and Developing Countries led by the Argentine law professor Carlos Correa, the TRIPS Agreement does not specify what an "invention" is, and since there is no "universal" concept of what it means, countries can, within certain limits, opt for various alternatives. "The scope of the concept can be determined by national legislation, in a broad or narrow sense. Thus, there is no obligation under the TRIPS Agreement to adopt an expansive concept of 'invention', as is currently done by many developed countries. In particular, nothing in the Agreement obliges Members to consider that substances existing in nature, biological or not, are patentable, even if isolated and claimed in a purified form" (Correa 2000: p 228).

Referring to Articles 27.2 and 27.3, the Expert Group also states that several exclusions from patentability may be provided for and this is an area where developing countries also enjoy some room for manoeuvre. According to the Group's report: "The ethical, economic and legal implications for allowing the patenting of plants and animals (as well as parts thereof), even if genetically altered, strongly indicate that these should be subject to a clear exclusion from patentability." It adds that there is an obligation under the TRIPS Agreement to grant patents on micro-organisms. "However, this obligation may be interpreted as applicable only to genetically modified organisms, and not to those existing in nature" (Correa 2000: p 230).

The lack of consistency and rationale for the distinctions has become a major issue in the WTO itself. In August 1999, as part of the preparatory process for the WTO's Seattle Ministerial Conference, Kenya on behalf of the African Group submitted a detailed paper to the General Council on the TRIPS Agreement (Kenya 1999). This paper has become a landmark document that lays out the position of a large number of developing countries on the confusing distinctions made in Article 27.3(b), as well as concrete proposals for amending the Article.

According to the paper: "There is a lack of clarity on the criteria/rationale used to decide what can and cannot be excluded from patentability in Article 27.3(b). This relates to the artificial distinction made between plants and animals (which may be excluded) and micro-organisms (which may not be excluded); and also between 'essentially biological' processes for making plants and animals (which may be excluded) and microbiological processes. By stipulating compulsory patenting of micro-organisms (which are natural living things) and microbiological processes (which are natural processes), the provisions of Article 27.3 contravene the basic tenets on which patent laws are based: that substances and processes that exist in nature are a discovery and not an invention and thus are not patentable. Moreover, by giving Members the option whether or not to exclude the patentability of plants and animals, Article 27.3(b) allows for life forms to be patented.

"The review of the substantive provisions of Article 27.3(b) should clarify the following:

- Why the option of exclusion of patentability of plants and animals does not extend to micro-organisms as there is no scientific basis for the distinction.
- Why the option of exclusion of patentability of 'essentially biological processes' does not extend to 'microbiological processes' as the latter are also biological processes.

"The review process should clarify that plants and animals as well as micro-organisms and all other living organisms and their parts cannot be patented, and that natural processes that produce plants, animals and other living organisms should also not be patentable."

In a subsequent paper on its own behalf, presented at a TRIPS Council meeting in September 2000, Kenya extended the logic of the August 1999 paper, by proposing that Article 27.3(b) be amended to take into account the concerns raised. According to the Kenyan statement, the amendments should "prohibit or exclude from patentability all biological and living organisms (these include plants, animals, micro-organisms and parts thereof such as cells, cell lines, genes and genomes) as well as any processes making use of, or relating to, such biological and living organisms. This prohibition is justifiable on legal, scientific, developmental, moral and ethical grounds" (Kenya 2000: p 7).

The inappropriateness of the patent system as a method for rewarding innovation in the field of biological sciences or in relation to biological materials and processes has been pointed out by some scientists (Shiva 1995a; Tewolde 1999b; Ho and Traavik 1999). In a paper on this subject, the African scientist (and general manager of the Ethiopian Environment Authority) B.G.E. Tewolde (2001) states that TRIPS gives no reason why useful human interventions in machines and living things, which everybody knows are different, should be rewarded through the same system. The problem is "with the criteria for granting patents, which were developed as appropriate for tools and machines, being extended blindly into the realm of living things." The problems which arise from the differences between machines and living organisms are exacerbated by the lack of precision in the provisions, since TRIPS does not define many of the important terms. Tewolde argues that in the TRIPS provision on "patentable subject matter" (Article 27.1), the term "invention" and the distinction between "product" and "process" make the patenting system inappropriate for life forms and life processes. The argument is as follows.

Firstly, no living thing has been obtained by human agency constructing it solely out of the non-living world, and thus life or living organisms cannot be considered an "invention." Several examples of inappropriate patenting are given: (i) Finding a hitherto "unknown" trait or traits, which is patentable in some countries, is a "discovery", not "invention." (ii) Determining the nucleic acid sequence of a gene is also said to enable patenting in some countries, but whether the sequence is known to anyone will not make the slightest difference to the traits of the organism and such sequencing is thus merely a discovery and should not be patentable. (iii) When a specific gene (a nucleic acid sequence) is introduced into an organism, the introduced gene may be expressed (i.e., it may result in a trait new to that receiving organism). But just as the gene existed in another organism, so did the trait it determines. Neither the introduced gene nor the expressed trait are inventions and they should thus not be patentable. (iv) The expression of the introduced gene is not always as predicted as its expression in its new host organism may be different from its expression in its parent organism. It would be a discovery, not an invention, and thus not patentable. (v) The use of specific biomolecules is also being patented in some countries. However, the extraction of biomolecules from living things is obviously a discovery, not an invention, since the biomolecules existed prior to being extracted. Since the biomolecule existed before extraction, its properties also existed before extraction. The use of a biomolecule is simply the result of recognising one existing useful property of the biomolecule; patenting that use is thus inconsistent with the criteria for determining what constitutes an "invention" (Tewolde 2001).

Secondly, mechanical and biological processes are fundamentally different. For example, a combination of hands, tools and machines is used to make a carburettor. In contrast, after the introduction of a gene into an organism and the resulting production of a transgenic organism, "the process of living takes over from the transgenic individual and makes it produce many more transgenic individuals through reproduction. This extra process has no mechanical counterpart or analogue." It is not caused by the introduction of the foreign gene, but is something that is common to all life. This process substitutes in each generation for the hands, tools and machines needed to make each carburettor. Even if the distinction between "invention" and "discovery" is ignored, it is not logical or fair to consider that the person concerned has "invented" any generation beyond that particular individual into which the foreign gene was originally introduced. "The reproduction process, so essential to genetic engineering 'products', thus wipes out every 'invention'" (Tewolde 2001).

Tewolde concludes that discoveries relating to life forms and processes, though not inventions, should also be rewarded. "A system for such rewards should be developed. However, distorting the meaning of patenting in order to make it applicable to life only serves to attract the rejection of the whole system. Who ever worried about the legitimacy of patenting before the 1990s, before it became known that the USA was allowing the patenting of living things? But now, opposition is growing all the time, opposition not only to the legitimacy, but also to the legality, of patenting."

The case against the patenting of naturally occurring organisms should be clear, since there is neither novelty nor invention involved. The Indian scientist and environmentalist, Vandana Shiva, argues that even in the case of genetically-engineered organisms, the claim for patentability is wrong, as it is "based on the false assumption that genes make organisms and therefore makers of transgenic genes make transgenic organisms. This is false because genes do not make organisms. Proteins are not made by genes but by a complex system of chemical production involving other proteins. They cannot make themselves any more than they can make a protein. Genes are made by a complex machinery of proteins. It is also not genes that are self-replicating but the entire organism as a complex system. Since the entire organism is self-replicating, and not the genes alone, relocating genes does not amount to making an entire organism. The organism 'makes' itself. To claim that an organism and its future generations are products of an 'inventor's mind' needing to be protected by IPRs as biotechnological inventions amounts to denying the self-organising, self-replicating structures of organisms. Put simply, it amounts to a theft of nature's creativity" (Shiva 1995a: p 6).

In a joint paper on a scientific briefing on TRIPS, Dr Mae-Wan Ho and Dr Terje Traavik comment that Article 27.3(b) is couched in undefined terms, designed to allow the broadest categories of patents from genetic engineering and other new biotechnologies. They argue that all classes of new biotech patents should have been rejected on one or more of the following grounds: all involve biological processes not under the direct control of the scientist and cannot be regarded as inventions; there is no scientific basis to support the patenting of genes and genomes, which are discoveries at best; the hit-or-miss technologies associated with many of the "inventions" are hazardous to health and biodiversity; many patents involve acts of plagiarism of indigenous knowledge and biopiracy of plants and animals bred and used by local communities for millennia; a range of patents are unethical (as they contribute to destruction of livelihoods, contravene basic human rights and dignity, compromise healthcare, impede medical and scientific research or are otherwise contrary to public order and morality).

Four classes of patents which Ho and Traavik consider should not be allowed are as follows:

(i) Patents on processes for which claims are wrongly made for novelty and invention. These include patents on extracts of plants developed and used for millennia by indigenous communities for the purposes claimed in the patents, for example patents on extracts of the neem plant used in India and other countries, and extracts of the bibiru and cunani used by the Wapixana Indians of North Brazil.
(ii) Patents on discoveries, such as micro-organisms, cell lines, genomes and genes which are derived from naturally occurring organisms.
(iii) Patents on transgenic techniques and constructs, and transgenic plants, animals and micro-organisms resulting from the techniques, which are being constructed as inventions and patentable in some countries.
(iv) Patents on nuclear-transplant cloning and other *in vitro* reproductive techniques (that, for example, produced Dolly the sheep) and organisms resulting from those techniques.

On the distinctions made in Article 27.3(b), Ho and Traavik state: "As ***all*** biotech processes are biological, they should be excluded from patenting, and this applies also to microbiological processes. There is no sound reason to regard microbiological as anything but biological. Also, micro-organisms ***are*** organisms, so there is no reason to treat them as patentable when plants and animals are excluded."

In particular, the scientists question the patentability of genes or nucleic acid (DNA or RNA) sequences. Such patentability is sought to be justified on the ground that they have been subject to a microbiological or non-biological process (i.e., gene sequencing, which is itself a standard process that is patentable or already patented); thus the actual patented entity is the nucleic acid sequence itself and its putative function. Ho and Traavik point out two major problems with such patenting. Firstly, the DNA or RNA sequence is subject to change by mutation, deletion, insertion and rearrangement. This raises the issue: if the original sequence is patented, does it mean that variously mutated sequences are no longer covered? Secondly, the patentability based on function is problematic. "Industrial application" involves the functional side of the gene sequence, and presumably qualifies it as an invention. However, the nucleic acid molecule by itself can do nothing and can only have a function in a living cell or an organism. But its function is uncertain and unpredictable as it depends on which kind of cell it is in, where in the genome it is inserted, in what kind of genome and in which environment. "For example, the acetyl-CoA carboxylase gene, which confers herbicide resistance in monocots, is claimed primarily for regulating oil content in a patent. Under some circumstances, again beyond the control of the genetic engineer, the gene is silenced, so it has no function whatsoever. Thus, the patentability based on function is equally unscientific" (Ho and Traavik 1999).

3. PROTECTION OF PLANT VARIETIES

Article 27.3(b) of TRIPS also obliges member countries to provide for the protection of plant varieties. This they may do either by patents or by an "effective *sui generis* system" or by any combination of these.

Prior to the establishment of the TRIPS Agreement, most developing countries had not granted patents for living organisms and neither did they have a system for the protection of plant varieties. There has instead been a tradition of free exchange of seeds and genetic materials in the farming communities. Many developed countries, which also traditionally did not patent living organisms, protected plant varieties through legislation establishing plant breeders' rights, which was aimed at protecting the work of plant breeders. Most countries that have established plant breeders' rights have joined the UPOV (International Union for the Protection of New Varieties of Plants) which has a convention aimed at granting exclusive intellectual property rights to breeders of new plant varieties. The latest revisions of the convention were in 1978 and 1991.

Due to their having to fulfil their TRIPS obligations, developing countries no longer have the option of not having a system of protection for plant varieties. They now have to choose between patenting or an "effective" *sui generis* system, and if they opt for a *sui generis* system, they then have to choose between possible *sui generis* systems. One problem they may anticipate is the interpretation of the term "effective." It is probable that some developed countries would interpret "effective" to mean that the *sui generis* system would, like the UPOV 1991 model, afford a similar level or type of protection to plant breeders and corporations as the patenting system. However, since there is no definition given on what "effective" means, each country is at liberty to set up its own system and make an argument for why it meets the test of "effectiveness."

Whilst previously no country granted patents for living organisms, patents are now increasingly given in the United States for plant varieties and agricultural products based on biotechnology. However, most developing countries have chosen not to use the patent option in plant variety protection.

As pointed out by Ghayur Alam (1999), the protection provided by plant breeders' rights is weaker compared to patents. But in recent years, there has been a trend towards increasingly strict protection of plant breeders' rights, such that they are approaching the standards of patenting. UPOV 1978 provides two important exemptions to breeders' rights: (i) breeders' exemption (allowing breeders to use protected varieties for breeding purposes and developing new varieties, including the freedom to exploit these new varieties commercially); and (ii) farmers' privilege (which allows farmers to save protected seeds for sowing in subsequent years). The UPOV convention was amended in 1991 to strengthen the position of plant breeders' rights holders as against other breeders and farmers: (i) The scope of breeders' exemption was reduced. Whilst researchers can still make use of protected material for research, a new variety cannot be used for commercial purposes if it is essentially derived from a protected variety, or if its production requires repeated use of a protected variety. (ii) The scope of farmers' privilege was also reduced. Whilst the privilege was automatic in UPOV 1978, a state joining UPOV 1991 has to make a special provision in its national law to include farmers' privilege. Also, these privileges must be "within reasonable limits and subject to the safeguarding of the legitimate interests of the breeder" (Ghayur Alam 1999: pp 2-3).

Since the option of signing on to the 1978 convention is now closed, countries that have not yet joined UPOV and would like to do so would have to sign on to the UPOV 1991 convention. In so doing, they would have to agree to adopt the stricter protection standards for plant breeders' rights.

Several studies (including Gaia and GRAIN 1998b; Nijar 1999a) have highlighted the possible negative consequences for developing countries in joining UPOV, especially on the basis of the 1991 convention. The most serious problem is the curtailment of farmers' rights. It is pointed out that UPOV denies farmers' rights in the narrow sense (the right to freely save seed from the harvest is curtailed) and the wider sense (UPOV does not recognise or support communities' inherent rights to biodiversity and their space to innovate) (Gaia and GRAIN 1998b: p 10). According to Nijar (1999a: pp 1-2), the right of farmers to save seeds for their own use is severely restricted in three ways: firstly, countries are to allow this "within reasonable limits and subject to the safeguarding of the legitimate interests of the breeder"; secondly, the farmer must only use the seeds for propagating purposes on his own holding; thirdly, the prohibition extends to seeds that are essentially derived. "This effectively ends farmers' traditional right and customary practice of saving, using, exchanging seeds and sharing or selling, his farm produce."

The UPOV system also discriminates against and undermines the context of traditional and local innovation and breeding as the definition of innovation relies on an industrial perspective of professionals innovating for commercial advantages. There is lack of appreciation of what is a useful plant variety from the farmers' perspective or its value for sustainability (Gaia and GRAIN 1998b: p 7). The UPOV 1991 model also discourages innovation by other plant breeders, who are now prohibited from using a new variety for commercial purposes if it is "essentially derived" from a protected variety.

Moreover, the UPOV criteria for protection also encourage the process by which genetic erosion takes place, as powerful commercial breeders obtain the right to IPRs-sanctioned monopolies, and this right is given only if the variety is genetically uniform. The uniformity and stability requirements in UPOV stimulate breeders to work with "elite germplasm" and to produce a limited range of similar seeds. This contributes to the process of the replacement of genetically-diverse and traditional varieties by genetically-uniform modern seeds (Gaia and GRAIN 1998b: p 5).

TRIPS does not specify that the *sui generis* option must be met by joining UPOV. Thus, WTO members can choose their own *sui generis* system of plant variety protection. Some developing countries have joined UPOV and signed on to the 1978 or 1991 conventions. However, the concerns listed above, especially the effect of restriction on farmers' rights, have caused many developing countries to have reservations about joining UPOV, especially its 1991 convention. Thus, many countries have not joined (or not yet joined) UPOV, and several of these countries are drafting their own national legislation on plant variety protection.

As pointed out by G.S. Nijar (1996), the terms of Article 27.3(b) of TRIPS allow flexibility for countries to provide for protection of plant resources by a model that is compatible with their culture and traditional practices. This could also protect the diverse knowledge systems in relation to plant and other genetic resources. "Legislation on the setting up of a *sui generis* system of protection for plant varieties can be developed by Third World countries which accords recognition to innovations of indigenous peoples and local communities and which is compatible with their social and cultural values and ethos. Such a protective system could, for example, define innovation to include any inventive input done collectively, accretionally, inter-generationally and over time in relation to genetic resources. Such an innovation would be protected even if the innovation is not intended for trade, fulfils a social purpose and serves the common good" (Nijar 1996: p 28).

Nijar further argues that this *sui generis* system would effectively protect ownership rights of farmers and indigenous peoples over their plant varieties and seeds, and if adopted by a sufficient number of countries, this legislation would prove to be widely effective and fulfil the requirement for an "effective *sui generis*" system. Moreover, countries would be fulfilling their obligations under the CBD, whose Article 8(j) obliges parties to respect, preserve and maintain knowledge, innovations and practices of indigenous and local communities (Nijar 1996: pp 28-29).

In another paper, Nijar (1999b) elaborates on the core elements of a possible *sui generis* law for plant varieties that would be consistent with several instruments, including the CBD, the Biosafety Protocol, UPOV 1978 and the exclusionary provisions of TRIPS. These elements include the following:

(i) It must recognise and protect the right of farmers and healers (indigenous peoples and local communities) over plant varieties developed by them, inter-generationally, collectively and for the social good. Their prior informed consent must be sought for the use of their variety, and no rights can be created in favour of breeders in respect of plant varieties derived from plants which are invested with the knowledge of indigenous peoples and local communities.

(ii) There must be recognition of this right without the need for registration. Proof of ownership will be in accordance with the customs and traditions of the particular indigenous peoples or local communities.

(iii) To qualify for recognition and protection, the variety must be identifiable; this should be the only criterion.

(iv) Breeders' rights should not extend beyond the production for the purposes of commercial marketing, the offering for sale and the marketing of the reproductive or vegetative propagating material as such of the variety.

(v) In particular, the breeders' rights should not extend to the harvested crop of a small farmer growing the breeders' protected plant variety.

(vi) The concept of "essentially derived variety" should be limited such that it does not impair or stifle innovation.

(vii) Farmers should be entitled to save seeds for their own use and be entitled to use their harvest as further planting material.

(viii) There should be no approval of breeders' rights where the public interest so requires (such a restriction of rights is allowed under Article 9 of UPOV 1978 and Article 17 of UPOV 1991). Such a public interest may arise where biodiversity is adversely affected; where the variety poses a potential hazard to the agricultural system and to human, animal and plant life or health, based on the precautionary principle; where the variety does not possess the normal regenerative and reproductive capacity associated with the variety; where introduction of the variety may have an adverse socioeconomic impact or affect the innovative capacity and indigenous technologies of farmers, healers, indigenous peoples and local communities; where there are ethical reasons to reject the right.

(ix) Certain exclusions to the breeders' rights should be provided for (as permitted by Article 30 of TRIPS): acts done privately and for a non-commercial purpose; use of the variety for teaching purposes; use of the variety for research and experimentation; parallel imports of the variety on the principle of international exhaustion (Article 6 of TRIPS); exchange of propagating material between small farmers within defined limits; sale of farm-saved seeds in particular situations, for example, where the farmer cannot use his own seeds due to natural disasters or other unforeseen situations.

(x) A provision which allows for compulsory licensing (permitted by Article 31 of TRIPS) in certain situations, such as: where anti-competitive practices of the rights holders are identified; where food security may be affected; where a high proportion of the plant variety offered for sale is being imported; where the requirements of the farming community for propagating material of a particular variety are not met; where it is considered important to promote the public interest for socioeconomic reasons and for developing indigenous and other technologies.

In a model with the above elements, a country would be able to have a plant variety protection law that protects the rights of farmers and local communities that make use of their traditional resources and practices and which conforms to their customary exchange and use of seeds. The law also affords protection to breeders, giving them certain exclusive rights to new varieties, whilst also restricting these rights in various ways enumerated above. Thus, it is argued that this *sui generis* model would enable a country to work towards fulfilling its obligations in the CBD and, at the same time, being consistent with TRIPS.

In order to enable WTO members to more confidently embark on national legislation that protects the rights of farmers and local communities, it would be useful for the WTO to explicitly clarify that this principle (i.e., the protection of farmers' rights and local community rights) can be included as a vital component in the *sui generis* option.

In March 1996, the Indian delegation presented a paper at the WTO's Committee on Trade and Environment. In a section on plant variety protection, the paper stated: "As it now stands, Members are free to incorporate in their *sui generis* laws any measures for exclusion, revocation, use without the authorisation of the right holder, reduction in the term of protection and even for sharing of benefits with traditional communities, in the context of discouraging the production and use of plant varieties which are injurious to the environment and encouraging the production and use of those that safeguard or are beneficial to the environment, provided that these provisions are otherwise consistent with the TRIPS Agreement."

In its August 1999 paper on the TRIPS Agreement (Kenya 1999), the African Group proposed that the implementation of the provision in Article 27.3(b) in respect of plant varieties be clarified, so as to allow developing countries to:

(i) Meet their international obligations, for example under the CBD and the FAO International Undertaking for Plant Genetic Resources.
(ii) Satisfy their need to protect the knowledge and innovations in farming, agriculture and health and medical care of indigenous peoples and local communities. The resolution of this issue affects the food security, social and economic welfare, and public health of people in developing countries. These concerns are central and can be taken into account under Articles 7 and 8 of TRIPS.
(iii) Protect human, animal and plant life, and to avoid serious prejudice to the environment. Exclusions from patentability for these purposes are permitted under Article 27.2 of TRIPS.

The African Group paper then proposed that after the sentence on plant variety protection in Article 27.3(b), a footnote should be inserted that any *sui generis* law for plant variety protection can provide for:

(i) the protection of the innovations of indigenous and local farming communities in developing countries, consistent with the CBD and the International Undertaking on Plant Genetic Resources;
(ii) the continuation of the traditional farming practices including the right to save and exchange seeds, and sell their harvest;
(iii) preventing anti-competitive rights or practices which will threaten food sovereignty of people in developing countries, as permitted by Article 31 of the TRIPS Agreement.

This proposal articulates the essential concerns that African countries as well as several other developing countries (and also many environmental and development organisations) have in relation to the need to ensure that the implementation of the TRIPS Agreement does not undermine the rights, resources and knowledge of farmers, healers, indigenous and local communities in relation to biological diversity, and that moreover it is possible for WTO members to introduce their own legislation that establishes the rights of these communities, as well as the rights of plant breeders within certain limits.

4. CONCLUSIONS AND SUGGESTIONS

The issue of IPRs over biological materials and genetic resources has serious implications for sustainable development. There is serious concern among policy makers in many developing countries, and among many environment and development organisations, that Article 27.3(b) of the TRIPS Agreement and its implementation will open the door to an eventual flood of patents on life forms: plants, animals and even human beings and their parts, especially those that are genetically modified, and also even including some biological materials or organisms that are naturally occurring. There is also a serious concern that even if plant varieties can be exempted from patentability, there will be a major push to have WTO members implement IPRs laws that afford strong protection to commercial plant breeders by giving them exclusive rights to plant varieties.

Should the concerns prove justified and the trend towards stronger IPRs protection continue, there are likely to be serious implications. The monopolisation of private and corporate rights over knowledge and biological materials will expand, thus eroding the rights and traditional practices of farmers and local communities. Since the majority of patents are registered in developed countries, and this trend is likely to continue, the balance of benefits from the use and control of technology will shift even more from developing to developed countries as the IPRs system is applied to biological resources. This imbalance is even more unfair in the case of biodiversity, since the origin of genetic resources and knowledge of their use are mainly located in developing countries. The appropriation by corporations and other developed-country institutions (through the IPRs regimes) of local and traditional knowledge originating in communities of developing countries is particularly unjustifiable.

The effects on the environment would also be serious. For example:

(i) The adoption of the patent regime will intensify the trend of private monopolisation of knowledge and genetic resources. This would make it more difficult for researchers to make use of genetic material for research aimed at devising environmentally more suitable ways of cultivation and production.

(ii) Patenting of life forms would tremendously increase the profit opportunity for biotechnology firms to introduce and commercialise genetically-engineered crops and materials. As the technology is backed up by powerful corporations with the means to push the technology and its products over an increasing share of crop acreage, the acreage of traditional varieties with wider range of diversity will correspondingly be reduced. There is also increasing scientific evidence that the large-scale commercialisation of genetically-engineered crops can lead to loss of biodiversity through the "genetic contamination" of relatives.

(iii) If patenting or the dominant system of plant breeders' rights is increasingly applied, this will also encourage greater uniformity of plant varieties and erode genetic diversity in agriculture. The UPOV criteria of uniformity and stability give an incentive to breeders to work only with "elite" germplasm, or to recycle familiar breeding materials and produce variations on a theme. Less than 7 percent of the germplasm used by professional breeders is "exotic" as there is no pressure on breeders to develop genetically broader varieties; instead, there is a push to focus on single genes making the difference between one variety and another. Farmers are thus being offered similar seeds, and the eroding genetic base could potentially lead to crop losses (Gaia and GRAIN 1998b: p 5).

In respect of Article 27.3(b) of TRIPS, a review process is currently being undertaken in the TRIPS Council. The review should seriously consider whether the patent system is an appropriate reward system for innovations in the area of living organisms and biological materials. As pointed out by some experts, the patent system was designed for mechanical inventions and objects, and is it is unsuitable to apply it to living organisms. Thus, applying patents to living organisms distorts the patent system. Other, more appropriate ways of rewarding innovations in this field should thus be sought. In any case, the rationale (or lack thereof) for the distinctions made in Article 27.3(b) between plants and animals and micro-organisms and between biological and microbiological processes has to be clarified and the seeming contradiction resolved; at the least, it could be clarified that all naturally occurring living organisms are not patentable. The status of patentability of genetically-modified organisms is less clear. Even if a country were to decide in its law that such organisms are an "invention", it does not follow that all countries have to adopt the same definition or come to the same conclusion. Countries should thus be free to make their own decision on patentability of all kinds of life forms and processes.

As for plant varieties, most developing countries had not until recently applied IPRs. The review process could clarify that countries have the flexibility to choose the protection system they deem appropriate to protect the rights of those groups or individuals that are to be recognised as innovators and owners of knowledge. The review process could even determine that each country can choose whether or not an intellectual property regime is needed for plant varieties, especially since most countries did not (or still do not) have such protection. If protection is still to be required, then under the *sui generis* option, countries should be entitled to adopt a system that maximally protects the rights of farmers and local communities, in ways that preserve and encourage their knowledge, practices and systems of innovation, and which enables the continued or increased conservation of biodiversity.

Chapter 5

IPRs, TRIPS and Technology Transfer

1. TECHNOLOGY TRANSFER IN THE "ENVIRONMENT AND DEVELOPMENT" PROCESS

THE need for transfer of environmentally sound technology (EST) to developing countries has for a long time been seen as one of the major aspects of the process of sustainable development. During the 1992 United Nations Conference on Environment and Development (UNCED) in Rio de Janeiro and the process leading to it, technology transfer and financial resources were the two major cross-cutting issues, and constituted the two main demands of the developing countries.

In the UNCED negotiating process, the key issue in technology transfer was IPRs. The Group of 77 countries argued that IPRs had to be relaxed in the case of EST, for otherwise IPRs would hinder the developing countries' access to such technology.

The developed countries' delegations were very sensitive on this point and refused to concede. Whilst agreeing that concessional terms should be encouraged for the transfer of ESTs, they insisted that IPRs (such as patents) be applied and that an exception should not be made in IPRs regimes on such technologies.

Finally, the chapter on technology in Agenda 21 (a programme of action for sustainable development adopted at UNCED) called for action to promote and finance the access to and transfer of ESTs to developing countries on favourable (including concessional and preferential) terms. But it also says these terms must be "mutually agreed" upon and also take into account the need to protect IPRs.

The full application of such rights would be a major barrier to technology transfer, and deprive the commitment to transfer technology of much of its content. There is thus a fundamental tension within the agreement on technology, and room for more discussion on how to operationalise the Agenda 21 proposals on technology cooperation, transfer and capacity building. The developing countries consider this to be an area where assistance from the developed countries is critically needed.

2. IPRs AND TECHNOLOGY TRANSFER

Since Rio, there has also been little or no progress on facilitating the transfer of EST to the South. At the United Nations Commission on Sustainable Development, a working group on technology transfer was set up in 1993, but after a few years the group was closed down, signifying the erosion and loss of importance the subject has suffered. Instead of the concessions asked for by developing countries, the reverse trend towards much stricter IPRs regimes (including for EST) prevailed, when the TRIPS Agreement came into force together with the WTO in 1995.

Proponents of a strict IPRs regime have argued that it would encourage innovation and contribute to technology transfer. Opponents point out that granting exclusive rights to IPRs holders would enable them to monopolise the technology, hinder research by other parties and prevent the use by and spread to other parties.

At international policy fora, developed countries have been taking the pro-IPRs position whilst developing countries have generally raised concerns about the negative effects of a strict IPRs regime on technology transfer.

In relation to the environment, some technologies can have a negative impact whilst others may have a positive impact. It would be rational for policy frameworks (whether at national or international levels) to recognise the need to discourage the former whilst encouraging the latter.

In so far as the granting of IPRs provides an incentive for developing technologies, then the ability to prohibit IPRs for environmentally-damaging technologies should be part of the policy armoury of a government. The TRIPS Agreement recognises this point (see Section 4 below).

In relation to EST, there is a strong case that IPRs hinder the ability of developing countries to attain EST as well as new technologies in general. To begin with, the great majority of patents are held by companies based in North America, Western Europe or Japan. As Oh (2000a) points out: "Only 3 percent of world patents are owned by inventors in the developing countries. Specifically, the vast majority of biotech patents are in the name of companies originating in the developed countries. A survey of the biotechnology patents showed that between 1990-1995, around 25,000 patents were granted throughout the world. Thirty-seven percent of these originated in the US, a similar percentage from Japan, whilst 19 percent were from the European Union. The remaining 7 percent of patents came from the 'rest of the world', including all of the developing countries."

It is sometimes argued that a strong IPRs regime in a country will encourage the inflow of foreign direct investment (FDI), which in turn will bring about technology transfer to the host country. However, according to an UNCTAD study on TRIPS and developing countries: "To date, there is little conclusive evidence that strengthened intellectual property protection would consistently expand the transfer of technology to developing countries. Key determinants of technology transfer (through FDI and through arm's-length licensing) include the costs of making such transfers, which depend on local technological capability. This capability refers to factors such as skill availability, technology supply structures, R&D capacity, enterprise-level competence and institutional and other supporting technological infrastructures" (UNCTAD 1996: p 18).

By strengthening IPRs in developing countries, the TRIPS Agreement can also encourage foreign firms to import technology at higher prices rather than produce it in the host country, and also enable technology suppliers to raise their prices. These two factors raise the cost and reduce the flow of technology to developing countries. As pointed out by the same UNCTAD study, TRIPS limits the ability of countries to impose working requirements and issue compulsory licences; "a worrying implication of this limitation is that foreign firms may choose not to license technologies under the stronger IPR regime, but rather supply markets with imports at higher prices." Another negative effect on costs is that "technology-supplying firms will have stronger leverage in their bargaining positions as a result of stronger patent and trademark protection, permitting them to negotiate higher licence charges and royalty fees. Thus developing countries could suffer reduced inward technology flows at higher prices" (UNCTAD 1996: p 18).

According to Oh (2000a), there is concern that the use of IPRs may, in fact, adversely affect the flow of FDI. Analysis of the use of patents by foreign companies in developing countries has shown that such multinational corporations use patents as a "defensive strategy" (Dasgupta 1999). This refers to the use of patenting to preserve markets that were once captured through exports and are subsequently threatened by competitors and/or by the import-substituting strategies of the host countries.

In this context, therefore, patents do not provide the stimulus for foreign investment. Instead, in this situation, patents are used as instruments to achieve control over foreign markets, even without direct investment (thus eliminating the need for FDI). For this reason, studies have shown that approximately two-thirds of patented products are never produced. They are patented in order to keep rivals away from the field (Dasgupta 1999). The patent systems of some countries recognise the need to prevent such use of patenting. One of the objectives of the Indian patent law, for example, is the need to prevent registration of patents merely to enable patentees to enjoy monopoly for the importation of the patented article (Oh 2000a).

There are several ways in which a strong IPRs regime can hinder access of developing countries to technology, and transfer to developing countries of technology (including EST).

Firstly, a strict IPRs regime can discourage research and innovation by locals in a developing country. Where most patents in the country are held by foreign inventors or corporations, local R&D can be stifled since the monopoly rights conferred by patents could restrict the research by local researchers. Strict IPRs protection, by its apparent bias, may actually slow the pace of innovation in developing countries, and increase the knowledge gap between industrial and developing countries. In such situations, the IPRs system favours those who are producers of proprietary knowledge, vesting them with greater bargaining powers over the users (Oh 2000a).

As pointed out by Dr Ghayur Alam (1999): "The proposed changes to the IPR policies of developing countries have raised a number of important issues. One of the most important of these is the likely impact of these changes on a developing country's ability to undertake research and development in agriculture. We are particularly concerned about the impact of a strong IPR system on research aimed at the development of new plant varieties and genetically engineered plants." In relation to biotechnology research, Dr Ghayur states: "The research in this area is completely dominated by firms in developed countries, while public sector research institutions (both international and national) are very weak. The adoption of an IPRs system which includes patents for biotechnology-based techniques and products will be extremely detrimental to local research. As our study of cotton and rice research in India has shown, most of the important techniques and genes used in the development of genetically engineered plants are already owned by firms in developed countries. As these patent rights are not applicable in developing countries, local researchers are able to undertake research on local problems. However, once these rights become applicable in developing countries, research and its commercialisation will face serious problems."

Secondly, a strict IPRs regime makes it difficult for local firms or individual researchers to develop or make use of patented technology, as this could be prohibited or expensive.

Thirdly, should a local firm wish to "legally" make use of patented technology, it would usually have to pay significant amounts in royalty or licence fees. As pointed out earlier, TRIPS increases the leverage of technology suppliers to charge a higher price for their technology. Many firms in developing countries may not be able to afford the cost. Even if they could, the additional high cost could make their products unviable. Moreover, there could be a large drain on a developing country's foreign exchange as a result of having to pay foreign IPRs holders for the use of their technology. Many developing countries with serious debt problems will be unable to afford the cost of using the technologies.

Fourthly, even if a local firm is willing to pay the commercial rate for the use of patented technology, the patent holder can withhold permission to the firm or impose onerous conditions, thus making it impossible or extremely difficult for the technology to be used by the firm.

This can hinder progress of developing countries towards the use of EST. Holders of the patents to such technologies, which are usually Northern-centred transnational companies, can refuse to grant permission to companies in the South to use the technologies, even if they are willing to pay market prices; or onerous conditions are imposed; or else the technologies may be made available only at high prices (due to the monopoly enjoyed by the patent holders). Companies in the South may not be able to meet the conditions or afford to pay such prices, and if they do their competitiveness could be affected. As a result, developing countries may find difficulties in meeting their commitments to phase out the use of polluting substances under international environment agreements, such as the Montreal Protocol.

3. CASE STUDY OF EFFECT OF IPRs ON IMPLEMENTATION OF THE MONTREAL PROTOCOL

Local firms in some developing countries are finding it difficult to have access to substitutes for chlorofluorocarbons (CFCs), chemicals used in industrial processes as a coolant, which damage the atmosphere's ozone layer. This hinders their ability to meet commitments under the Montreal Protocol, an international agreement aimed at tackling ozone-layer loss by phasing out the use of CFCs and other ozone-damaging substances by certain target dates.

Under the Montreal Protocol, developed countries originally agreed to eliminate production and use of CFCs by the year 2000, whilst developing countries are given a 10-year grace period to do the same. A fund was set up to help developing countries meet the costs of implementing their phase-out, and the protocol's Article 10 provides for technology transfer to developing countries. Each party is obliged to take every practical step to ensure that the best available and environmentally safe substitutes and related technologies are expeditiously transferred to developing countries, under fair and most favourable conditions.

A study of the effect of IPRs on technology transfer in the case of India in the context of the Montreal Protocol has been conducted by Watal (1998). She points out that technology-transfer provisions in the Montreal Protocol are particularly relevant for developing countries which are producers of ozone-depleting substances (ODS), such as India, Brazil, China, South Korea and Mexico. In India, Korea and China, such production is dominated by local-owned firms, for which the access to ozone-friendly technology on affordable terms has become a central issue of concern. The study concludes that: "Efforts at acquiring substitute technology have not been successful as the technologies are covered by IPRs and are inaccessible either on account of the high price quoted by the technology suppliers and/or due to the conditions laid down by the suppliers. This would require domestically owned firms to give up their majority equity holding through joint ventures or to agree to export restrictions in order to gain access to the alternative technology." Moreover, financial assistance to acquire the technology was also not effective. A report of the executive committee on technology transfer of the protocol stated that the terms of freely-negotiated technology transfers, including costs such as patents, designs and royalties, may not always be accommodated by the Multilateral Fund's funding policies. "Thus, while prices of alternative technologies are unaffordable on account of IPRs, access to these is limited due to inadequate funds domestically and lack of financial assistance from the Multilateral Fund, creating a major hurdle in transiting to ozone-friendly production, especially among producer nations. For ODS producer countries with domestically owned firms, therefore, technology transfer is a distinct and crucial issue in itself requiring immediate attention" (Watal 1998: pp 1-2).

Two specific cases from Watal's study show the acute problems faced by local firms in their attempts to access technology from suppliers who hold patents over the products.

CFCs, which are ozone-depleting, have been used in refrigerators and air-conditioners that are manufactured in India. In most major sub-sectors, two alternative substitutes (HFC 134a and hydrocarbon) are available. Most Indian refrigerator manufacturers would like to convert to using HFC 134a. Indian producers of CFCs are very keen to acquire the technology for making HFC 134a for domestic and export sale. However, their efforts to access the technology were unsuccessful. Only a few companies in the developed countries control the patents and trade secrets related to HFC 134a, and thus developing countries have to either pay high royalty fees to produce them locally or lose the local and international markets for this alternative. One of the Indian companies that sought to access the technology was quoted a very high price of US$25 million by a transnational company that produces HFC 134a and that holds a patent on the technology. The supplier also proposed two alternatives to the sale, namely, that the Indian firm allow the supplier to take majority ownership in a joint venture to be set up, or that the Indian firm agree to export restrictions on HFC 134a produced in India. Both options were unacceptable to the Indian company, while the quoted price was also unrealistically high as it was estimated that the technology fee should at most have been between US$2 and $8 million.

The ozone-depleting substance halon is used in fire extinguishers and many other products. India imported all the halon it required up to 1990. Since 1991 it has manufactured halon 1211 and since 1995-96 it developed the technology for halon 1301. Producers of fire protection systems would like to convert from using halon 1301 to HFC 227ea (commercially known as FM 200). India would like to produce this alternative locally. FM 200 is covered by a methods and composition patent filed by a US company in 1995 with a life of 20 years. It was filed in several countries including China, Korea and Russia (but not in India, which, up to the time of the study, did not allow such patents). According to industry sources, China and Russia succesfully developed the process for FM 200 through indigenous R&D but will be prevented from marketing the final product due to this patent. An additional problem is that the patent owner has imposed several restrictive conditions for FM 200, such as that the components used in the fire protection systems should have the approval of the Underwriters' Laboratory (UL) or Factory Mutual (FM) of the US, and the systems' design must meet the requirement of NFPA-2000 (USA) and the approval of UL and FM (USA); and the final inspection/ clearance of the system (including various tests following international standards) must meet the approval of UL and FM. The costs to India to produce the alternative to halon 1301 would include US$1.5 million for licence fees to produce alternatives just for the halon 1301 sub-sector and another US$1.4 million to convert halon portable systems to ODS-free systems. Indian firms that have tried to acquire the technology faced the problem not only of finance, but found that the owner of the patent was not interested in licensing the technology to wholly owned companies. The patent holder was interested only in joint ventures in which it would hold a majority share. The Indian firms did not want to divest their equity holding but only wanted to buy the technology. Thus, in the case of HFC 227ea as in the case of HFC 134a, the technology supplier, which also owned the patent, was unwilling to transfer the environmentally sound technology to India, not even on commercial terms. In such a situation where the alternative cannot be produced within the country, the users of halon 1301 even in strategic sectors such as defence and power plants will have to depend entirely on imports of HFC 227ea to meet their demands.

These examples show how much the developing countries have been put on the spot. They join international environmental agreements and commit themselves to taking painful steps to change their economic policies or production methods. Financial aid and technology transfer on fair and most favourable terms are promised during the hard negotiations, to persuade the South countries to sign on. Then, when the agreements come into force, the funds fall far short of the promised level, and technology transfer fails to materialise.

Meanwhile, in another forum like the WTO, other treaties such as TRIPS are negotiated which produce or contribute to an opposite effect, increasing the obstacles to developing countries' access to EST. Yet, when the time comes, the developing countries can be expected to be pressured to meet their full obligations, such as phasing out the use of CFCs (in the Montreal Protocol) or reducing emissions of greenhouse gases (in the Climate Change Convention). There is thus an unfair imbalance. The North does not (or does not adequately) meet its obligation to assist the South, and the South (when meeting its commitments), because of the lack of aid and technology, will face economic dislocation.

One remedy being proposed by some public interest groups and developing countries is to revise international laws on patents so that the full weight of IPRs is not applied to EST.

4. TRIPS, TECHNOLOGY AND THE ENVIRONMENT

(a) Major Concerns about Effects of TRIPS on the Environment

In the WTO's Committee on Trade and Environment, the topic "TRIPS and environment" is being discussed under two issues: the relationship of the TRIPS Agreement with access to and transfer of technology and the development of environmentally sound technology; and the relationship between the TRIPS Agreement and multilateral environmental agreements which contain IPRs-related obligations.

There are several concerns in relation to the potential effects of TRIPS on the environment, including the following:

(i) Will TRIPS encourage the spread of environmentally harmful technologies?
(ii) Will TRIPS discourage or even prevent the spread and transfer of environmentally sound technologies?
(iii) Will TRIPS ironically facilitate the transfer of knowledge on the use of biological resources from communities in developing countries to enterprises or institutions in developed countries without the former being rewarded whilst the latter are granted exclusive patent rights?

A framework of discussing the issues relating to TRIPS, technology and environment from the perspective of developing countries was interestingly provided at the Committee on Trade and Environment meeting in March 1996 in a paper presented by India (India 1996). The paper stated that the types of intellectual protection (IP) covered in TRIPS are relevant in this context: patents, plant variety protection, layout designs of integrated circuits and undisclosed information. Two types of technologies incorporating IP are distinguished: those that harm and those that benefit the environment. The use of the first should be discouraged, and the second encouraged, by the international community.

The Indian paper's section on patents stated that for technologies harmful to the environment, measures needed to discourage their global use may include exclusion from patentability (so that incentives are not given to generate such technologies) and ban of their use or commercial exploitation. The TRIPS Agreement recognises this reasoning in Article 27.2. For environmentally beneficial technologies, to encourage their global use, the paper proposes that some amendments or clarifications be made to the TRIPS Agreement. (These two points are elaborated on below.)

The paper also deals with layout designs of integrated circuits and protection of undisclosed information, and with plant variety protection.

It suggests that amendments to the TRIPS Agreement in Section 5 (Articles 27, 31, 32, 33), Section 6 (Articles 36, 37, 38) and Section 7 (Article 39), and an understanding on plant variety protection (Article 27), dispute settlement (Article 64) and undisclosed information (Article 39), may be required.

The Indian paper was an early submission to the work of the Committee on Trade and Environment on TRIPS and the environment and set a useful framework for discussions on the issue.

(b) Excluding the Patenting of Environmentally Harmful Technologies and Products

The need for countries to be able to prevent the granting of patents for environmentally harmful products or technologies is recognised in the TRIPS Agreement. Its Article 27.2 allows members to exclude from patentability "inventions, the prevention within their territory of the commercial exploitation of which is necessary to protect *ordre public* or morality, including to protect human, animal or plant life or health or to avoid prejudice to the environment, provided that such exclusion is not made merely because the exploitation is prohibited by their law."

However, WTO members that wish to make use of this provision to prevent the patenting of environmentally harmful technologies may face the disapproval of some other members that could contest whether the prohibited technologies constitute "prejudice to the environment" or whether the exclusion is needed to protect life and health. In other words, there can be a clash of interpretations as to whether a particular technology (for example, genetic engineering) or its products are harmful to the environment or to human, plant and animal life and health. The fear of a dispute and of being hauled up before a WTO dispute panel may to some extent discourage a WTO member from making use of this provision. Thus, whilst TRIPS does afford leeway for countries to exclude harmful technologies from patentability, the test of the usefulness of this flexibility will come when some members make use of this provision to exclude the patenting of certain technologies and are then challenged by other members.

(c) Relaxing IPRs Standards for Environmentally Sound Technologies

For environmentally beneficial technologies, to encourage their global use, and in cases where other measures for technology transfer are not possible, India proposed three points:

(i) To allow free production and use of such technologies as are essential to safeguard or improve the environment, members may have to exclude these technologies from patentability. Such an exclusion is not incompatible with TRIPS and may have to be incorporated through a suitable amendment.
(ii) For currently patented technologies, members may revoke patents already granted, if this is done in consonance with the Paris Convention and is subject to judicial review.
(iii) To encourage the use of environmentally beneficial technology, members should be allowed to reduce the term of patent protection from the present minimum of 20 years to, say, 10 years, "so as to allow free access to environmentally-beneficial technologies within a shorter period."

(d) TRIPS, Biological Resources and Plant Varieties

Another key aspect of technology transfer and IPRs is the TRIPS provision in relation to biological materials. It requires governments to afford patent protection for micro-organisms and microbiological processes. It also requires that IPRs on plant varieties be protected either through patenting or through an "effective *sui generis* system of protection." This raises concerns that the knowledge of Third World farmers and indigenous communities that has mainly contributed to the development of crops and the use of plants will not be legally recognised in the patent regime, whilst the corporations which genetically engineer biological resources will be unfairly rewarded. Here there are two concerns. Firstly, there is a reverse transfer of knowledge and technology (in relation to the knowledge and use of biodiversity) from the South to the North, for which the South is not compensated even as Northern corporations are granted patents. Secondly, developing countries would then have to purchase biotechnology products at high prices (which are facilitated by the patent protection) even though they are the place of origin of the very biological resources (and of the knowledge on their utilisation) used in biotechnology. This is likely to lead to higher cost of seeds and food products in developing countries.

Dealing briefly with plant variety protection under TRIPS and the environment in its March 1996 paper, India noted that IP protection can be provided either by patents or by an effective *sui generis* law. According to the paper: "As it now stands, members are free to incorporate in their *sui generis* laws any measures for exclusion, revocation, use without the authorisation of the right holder, reduction in the term of protection and even for sharing of benefits with traditional communities, in the context of discouraging the production and use of plant varieties which are injurious to the environment and encouraging the production and use of those that safeguard or are beneficial to the environment, provided that these provisions are otherwise consistent with the TRIPS Agreement." It urged the Committee on Trade and Environment to give this interpretation.

5. PROVISIONS IN TRIPS FOR TECHNOLOGY TRANSFER

The TRIPS Agreement has several references and provisions that deal with technology transfer.

Article 7, which contains the objectives of the agreement, states: "The protection and enforcement of intellectual property rights should contribute to the promotion of technological innovation and to the transfer and dissemination of technology, to the mutual advantage of producers and users of technological knowledge and in a manner conducive to social and economic welfare, and to a balance of rights and obligations."

Article 8 is on principles. One of the two principles (Article 8.2) is as follows: "Appropriate measures, provided that they are consistent with the provisions of this Agreement, may be needed to prevent the abuse of intellectual property rights by right holders or the resort to practices which unreasonably restrain trade or adversely affect the international transfer of technology."

Article 66.2 on least developed countries states: "Developed country Members shall provide incentives to enterprises and institutions in their territories for the purpose of promoting and encouraging technology transfer to least-developed country Members in order to enable them to create a sound and viable technological base."

Despite these and other provisions in TRIPS that seek to promote technology transfer, in reality little or nothing has been done by developed countries to either provide concessions to developing countries or provide incentives to (or impose obligations on) their enterprises and institutions to disseminate or transfer technology to developing countries. This has led to an erosion of confidence in the seriousness or sincerity of the developed countries to fulfil the technology-transfer obligations of TRIPS. For example, in a paper to the WTO's General Council and to the TRIPS Council, the Indian delegation stated: "There has been little effort to implement this provision (Article 66.2), raising doubts about the effectiveness of the Agreement to facilitate technology transfers" (India 2000a).

In the same paper, India recounted an earlier proposal it had made to the Committee on Trade and Environment, "that owners of environmentally sound technology and products shall sell such technologies and products at fair and most favourable terms and conditions upon demand to any interested party which has an obligation to adopt these under national law of another country or under international law." Developing countries access technologies usually through licences and technology transfer agreements. The paper points out that technology seekers in developing countries face serious difficulties in their commercial dealings with technology holders in developed countries. These difficulties include: (i) those arising from imperfections of the market for technology; (ii) those arising from lack of experience and skill of enterprises and institutions in developing countries in concluding legal arrangements for technology acquisition; (iii) government practices (legislative and administrative) in developed and developing countries which influence the implementation of national policies and procedures designed to encourage the flow of technology to, and its acquisition by, developing countries.

For the TRIPS provisions on technology transfer to be implemented, these difficulties have to be addressed. To overcome some of the difficulties, developing countries would need to build suitable safeguards in their domestic IPRs laws. Also, commercially viable mechanisms need to be established to address the problems and needs of enterprises or institutions in developing countries that want to acquire technology but find its cost prohibitive due to economies of scale and other reasons. Moreover, the high cost of technology makes it difficult for smaller and poorer developing countries to acquire technology on commercial terms. They can only acquire the needed technology through government-to-government negotiations and with financial aid provided either by developed countries' governments and other institutions, or by inter-governmental organisations. Another problem is the denial of dual-use technologies, even on a commercial basis, to developing countries; under this guise, a variety of technologies and products required for their growth process is being denied to developing countries. (India 2000a: pp 2-3).

In order that the TRIPS objectives, principles and provisions on technology transfer are made effective, a review of how to operationalise the relevant provisions of the TRIPS Agreement should be carried out. The obligations on developed countries to provide incentives to or oblige the enterprises or other institutions in their countries to transfer technology to developing countries could be made stronger, with regular reviews of the implementation. Relaxation of the standards of protection for environmentally sound technology should also be done, including through amendments to the agreement. Progress towards the goal of technology transfer is essential in order for there not to be a further loss of confidence in the TRIPS Agreement's purported objective of technology dissemination and transfer.

REFERENCES

ActionAid, 1999. "Crops and Robbers: biopiracy and the patenting of staple food crops." London: ActionAid.

Chang, Ha-Joon, 2000. "Intellectual property rights and economic development: historical lessons and emerging issues."

Correa, Carlos, 1997. "Technology transfer and sustainable development after the Uruguay Round." Penang: Third World Network.

Correa, Carlos, 1998. *Implementing the TRIPS Agreement: General context and implications for developing countries*. Penang: Third World Network

Correa, Carlos, 1999. "Technology transfer in the WTO Agreements." *Biotechnology and Development Review*, October 1999.

Correa, Carlos, 2000. *Intellectual Property Rights, the WTO and Developing Countries*. Penang: Third World Network.

Das, Bhagirath Lal, 1998. *The WTO Agreements: Deficiencies, Imbalances and Required Changes*. Penang: Third World Network.

Dasgupta, B., 1999. "Patent Lies and Latent Danger: A study of the political economy of patents in India." *Economic and Political Weekly*, April 17-24, 1999.

Dhar, Biswajit and Sachin Chaturvedi, 1999. "TRIPS and CBD: the widening gulf." *Biotechnology and Development Review*, October 1999.

Gaia and GRAIN, 1998a. "TRIPS versus CBD." Briefing Paper, April 1998. London: Gaia Foundation and GRAIN.

Gaia and GRAIN, 1998b. "Ten reasons not to join UPOV." Briefing Paper, May 1998. London: Gaia Foundation and GRAIN.

Ghayur Alam, 1999. "The impact of TRIPS on agricultural research in developing countries."

GRAIN, 2000. "Of patents and pirates." Briefing Paper, July 2000. Barcelona: GRAIN.

Guardian, the, 2000. "The Ethics of Genetics." Special Report on Patenting of Life, 15 November 2000. (www.guardianunlimited.co.uk/genes/).

Hara, Mariko, 1999. "Issue paper on TRIPS and environmental issues." Geneva: UNEP.

Ho, Mae-Wan and Terje Traavik, 1999. "Why we should reject biotech patents from TRIPS". Scientific briefing on TRIPS Article 27.3(b).

India, Government, 1996. "Trade-related aspects of intellectual property rights and the environment: a contribution by India." Paper submitted to WTO Committee on Trade and Environment.

India, Government, 2000a. "Proposals on intellectual property rights issues." Paper submitted to WTO, 12 July 2000. (IP/C/W/195).

India, Government, 2000b. "Protection of biodiversity and traditional knowledge – the Indian experience." Paper submitted to WTO, 14 July 2000. (WT/CTE/W/156).

Kenya, Government, 1999. "The TRIPS Agreement." Communication from Kenya on behalf of the African Group. Paper submitted to WTO, 6 August 1999. (WT/GC/W/302).

Kenya, Government, 2000. Paper submitted to WTO TRIPS Council, September 2000.

MASIPAG, 1998. "Biopiracy, TRIPS and the patenting of Asia's rice bowl." A collective NGO situationer on IPRs on rice, issued in May 1998 in Geneva by 14 NGOs, including MASIPAG, Manila.

Nijar, G.S., 1996. "TRIPS and Biodiversity: the threat and responses." Penang: Third World Network.

Nijar, G.S., 1999a. "*Sui generis* law for plant varieties: preserving the knowledge and creativity of traditional breeders."

Nijar, G.S., 1999b. "Legal and practical perspectives on *sui generis* options." *Third World Resurgence*, No. 106, June 1999.

Nijar, G.S., 1999c. "The main elements of a Community Rights Act." Penang: Third World Network.

OAU, 1999. "African model law for the protection of the rights of local communities, farmers and breeders, and for the regulation of access to biological resources." Addis Ababa: Organisation of African Unity.

Oh, Cecilia, 2000a. "IPRs and biological resources: implications for developing countries." Briefing Paper. Penang: Third World Network.

Oh, Cecilia, 2000b. "TRIPS and Biodiversity: some questions and answers." Briefing Paper. Penang: Third World Network.

RAFI, 1997. *Conserving indigenous knowledge: integrating two systems of innovation*. New York: RAFI and UNDP.

Raghavan, Chakravarthi, 1999. "Protecting IPRs of local and indigenous communities." *South-North Development Monitor (SUNS)*, No. 4529, 14 October 1999.

Shiva, Vandana, 1995a. "Patents on life forms: playing God?". *Third World Resurgence*, No. 57, May 1995.

Shiva, Vandana, 1995b. "TRIPping over life." *Third World Resurgence*, No. 57, May 1995.

Tansey, Geoff, 1999. "Trade, intellectual property, food and biodiversity." London: Quaker Peace Service.

Tauli-Corpuz, Victoria, 1999a. Indigenous Peoples' Caucus Statement, presented at the Roundtable on Intellectual Property and Traditional Knowledge, WIPO, Geneva, 2 November 1999.

Tauli-Corpuz, Victoria, 1999b. "TRIPS and its potential impacts on indigenous peoples." Manila: Tebtebba Foundation.

Tebtebba Foundation, 1999. "No to patenting of life! Indigenous peoples' statement on the TRIPS Agreement of the WTO."

Tewolde Egziabher, 1999a. "A short comparison of the Model Law with the CBD." *Third World Resurgence*, No. 106, June 1999.

Tewolde Egziabher, 1999b. "Patenting life is owning life." *Third World Resurgence*, No. 106, June 1999.

Tewolde Egziabher, 1999c. "The TRIPS agreement of the WTO and the Convention on Biological Diversity: the need for coordinated action by the South." *Third World Resurgence*, No. 106, June 1999.

Tewolde Egziabher, 2001. *The Inappropriateness of the Patent System for Life Forms and Processes*. Biodiversity, Knowledge and Rights Series No. 1. Penang: Third World Network.

Tewolde Egziabher and Sue Edwards, 2000. "The Convention on Biological Diversity – with some explanatory notes from a Third World perspective." Institute for Sustainable Development and Third World Network.

UNCTAD, 1996. "The TRIPS Agreement and developing countries." New York and Geneva: UNCTAD.

UNCTAD, 2000a. "Systems and national experiences for protecting traditional knowledge, innovations and practices." Background note by UNCTAD Secretariat, 22 August 2000 (TD/B/COM.1/EM.13/2) for expert meeting on traditional knowledge, October 2000.

UNCTAD, 2000b. "Recommendations to UNCTAD from indigenous groups in attendance." Paper submitted to UNCTAD expert meeting on traditional knowledge, October 2000.

UNCTAD, 2000c. "Draft outcome of the expert meeting." Document of the UNCTAD expert meeting on traditional knowledge, October 2000.

Watal, Jayashree, 1998. "The issue of technology transfer in the context of the Montreal Protocol: Case Study of India."

www.ingramcontent.com/pod-product-compliance
Ingram Content Group UK Ltd.
Pitfield, Milton Keynes, MK11 3LW, UK
UKHW020737280225
455688UK00012B/708